Joe Stahlkuppe

American Pit Bull Terriers/ American Staffordshire Terriers

Everything About Purchase, Housing, Care, Nutrition, and Health Care

Filled with Full-color Photographs

Illustrations by Michele Earle-Bridges

BARRON'S

2 CONTENTS

INTRODUCTION

The Common Misconception

Over the last two decades, no breed of dog has been more maligned and misunderstood than the American Pit Bull Terrier (APBT). Just hearing the name of the breed has been enough to send chills down the backs of some fairly knowledgeable dog owners, not to mention the fear that the name pit bull brings out in the average person.

Contrast this negative perception with the real American Pit Bull Terrier and the American Kennel Club's version of the APBT, the American Staffordshire Terrier (Amstaff). It is true that this breed was originally bred for fighting. It is true that the APBT/Amstaff is probably pound for pound the most powerful breed of dog ever developed. They do have an incredibly high pain threshold. It is also true that with all this power comes unparalleled canine athleticism. Perhaps the most ironic truth of all is that thousands upon thousands of well-adjusted, non-dog-fighting people and families would not own any dog other than an Amstaff or an American Pit Bull Terrier. These people will tell you that their APBT/Amstaff is a loyal, intelligent, clean, loving pet with an excellent temperament.

The Fighting Dog Heritage

The American Pit Bull Terrier and the Amstaff originally came about as an experi-

APBT/Amstaffs are true canine athletes whose shady reputations are not borne out in reality—most make excellent pets.

ment in dog breeding to produce a fighting dog of speed, power, and exceptional grit or gameness (the ability to withstand pain). The dog breeders accomplished what they sought to do. Depending on which expert you listen to, the bull-and-terrier fighting dogs have been around for well over a hundred years.

The Great Dane was originally a boar hound. The Fox Terrier was originally bred to go into underground dens to fight with foxes and run them out. The Bull Mastiff was originally a gamekeeper's dog used to bring down poachers. None of these breeds do these original tasks today. A huge majority of American Pit Bull Terriers and American Staffordshire Terriers do not now do what they were originally bred to do either. These dogs have been tarred with the brush of public mistrust that has been based on the actions of a "sport" that was outlawed nearly a century ago. The fact that some diehards continue it still has had an impact on the breed.

Their Recent Bad Reputation and How It Happened

Ironically, even with all the bad publicity, the American Pit Bull Terrier/Amstaff is a very popular dog. With popularity comes a group of would-be dog breeders who want to cash in. Dogs that should never have been bred, even once, are bred repeatedly regardless of bad temperaments, health problems, or genetic defects—problems that, unfortunately, occur in every breed. Overbreeding of poor-quality dogs will ultimately hurt any breed.

The American Pit Bull Terrier has become popular with some people for all the wrong reasons. The general public heard all the horror stories about this "canine monster," and some people just had to have one. The supply of poorly bred APBT/Amstaffs caught up with the demand for the meanest, toughest dog on the block. The rest became a self-fulfilling prophesy. People who should never have owned a dog were able to get dogs that should never have been bred.

Identity Crisis: Other Dogs to Share the Blame

The American Pit Bull Terrier and the American Staffordshire Terrier have been given the blame for many sins. Some of these were, in truth, committed by poorly bred, poorly trained, poorly socialized, or poorly owned APBTs or Amstaffs. Other misdeeds credited to the American Pit Bull Terrier have been done by other breeds or by dogs of mixed ancestry. This sword cuts both ways. Dogs of other breeds have also been mis-

taken for APBTs. A general public and a mass media with pit bull on their minds will often see what they expect to see.

Other breeds somewhat resemble the American Pit Bull Terrier or the American Staffordshire Terrier. Sometimes these dogs are blamed, or should be blamed, for bad actions attributed to pit bulls or Amstaffs. Boxers, American Bulldogs, Bull Terriers (the long-faced *Spuds McKenzie* party dog), and Bulldogs (the English sour mugs) have all been mistakenly branded as APBTs at one time or another. Even the more dissimilar Rhodesian Ridgebacks, Labrador Retrievers, Chinese Shar-peis (the ones with all the wrinkles), and Great Danes have sometimes been misidentified as being APBTs or Amstaffs.

The American Pit Bull Terrier and the American Staffordshire Terrier are certainly not the first dogs to bear the brunt of public mistrust or unwarranted media exposure. Many dog breeds have had their time in the barrel. The German Shepherd, greatly loved today as an ultimate family pet, search-and-rescue dog, and guide for the visually impaired, was once the victim of bad press when unknowing people thought of the breed as the German police dog.

The real qualities of the APBT/Amstaff will enable these dogs to weather the negative publicity and public opinion storm. Concerned breeders have begun what amounts to a canine reclamation project. They have joined together to demonstrate the working abilities of these unique animals, their good dispositions when

Other breeds are sometimes mistaken for the APBT/Amstaff (which is in the very center). Clockwise from the APBT's left are a Bull Terrier, Boxer, American Bulldog, Staffordshire Bull Terrier, and Boston Terrier.

properly schooled, their great versatility, and their bright and funny personalities. Friends of the American Pit Bull Terrier and the American Staffordshire Terrier are doing much to offset the years of exploitation that brought these dogs into a bad light.

Human Culprits

The American Pit Bull Terrier did not get a bad reputation all by itself. Quite a few humans have been guilty of a variety of misdeeds. Dog fighters have kept alive the image of the American Pit Bull Terrier as a savage killer. The breed-for-greed crowd that will mass-produce poor-quality APBT/Amstaffs and then sell them to unsuspecting and unprepared members of the public deserves a lot of this guilt. The ignorant or uncaring dog buyer who purchases a dog just to have the meanest dog on the block owns a lot of responsibility along with a liberal dose of stupidity. The irresponsible APBT owner who does not have his or her dog trained and under control shares some of the blame. The media members who used the words pit bull when they were not sure of the breed in order to sensationalize a dog bite or attack story should know better. Those in the general public who have passed judgment on an entire breed based on what was heard about a few dogs are as guilty as the rest!

A Canine Loose Cannon?

Is the American Pit Bull Terrier a breed out of control? Are all APBT/Amstaffs problems just waiting to happen? The answer to these questions is no. Some APBTs are out of control and dangerous, just as some dogs of other breeds are out of control or dangerous. To say that the vast

Amstaffs and APBTs—No Longer One Breed

Once it would have been quite correct to say that the American Staffordshire Terrier and the American Pit Bull Terrier were one and the same breed bearing only different names. Both breeds were from the same identical genetic backgrounds. They look almost identical. They were similar in temperament and demeanor. Today, these breeds are *not* the same. In the over half century that they have largely been bred separately gradually they have become two different breeds. Once they were sibling breeds and now they are more like cousins. This is especially true in the APBTs as recognized by the American Dog Breeders Association that has no place at all for the Amstaff. The AKC recognizes only the American Staffordshire Terrier and the United Kennel Club recognizes both the UKC registered APBT and the UKC registered Amstaff. For the purposes of this book, we will refer to the two breeds as APBT/Amstaffs.

majority of APBT/Amstaffs are out of control is certainly not true.

The right APBT/Amstaff chosen from a well-bred litter with parentage of good temperament, if well socialized and given good training, will not be any more of a problem than any other breed. In fact, such an APBT/Amstaff would probably be less of a problem! If the American Pit Bull Terrier or American Staffordshire Terrier were coming on the scene right now for the first time, perceptions would be vastly different! They would have no fighting-dog history or stigma. The breed would not have been hurt by overbreeding of poor-quality

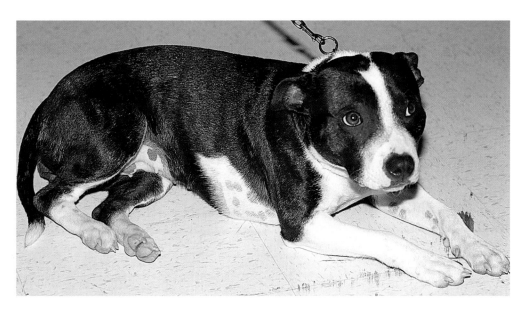

Above: This pup looks as if he may have done something wrong.

Below: An American Staffordshire wins a ribbon at an AKC show.

Left top: The APBT/Amstaff is commonly misunderstood due to its stern expression and intimidating appearance.

Left bottom: This puppy may be in charge of the truck, but he cannot seem to make his ears stay put.

Amstaffs and APBTs are usually easy to house-break and do well in obedience training. This breed could be said to be protective but is no more aggressive than many other breeds. The breed does not have a great many genetic

dogs. If you look at the APBT/Amstaff with fresh eyes, as if for the first time, you would see quite an exceptional breed of dog.

The Amstaff/APBT is of medium size. It has a short, easy-to-groom coat that comes in many attractive colors. The breed is large enough to be a good working terrier, but small enough to fit right in with most families in their homes.

problems. It is an attractive, versatile breed with many excellent qualities.

Is the APBT a loose canine cannon or an excellent all-around pet? That will depend largely on the dog's owner. If an owner takes time to find the right dog, carefully socializes it, thoroughly trains it, and provides for it in a responsible way, the odds are greatly in the favor of the Amstaff/American Pit Bull Terrier being a superb pet. With the wrong owner, the American Staffordshire Terrier or APBT could be among the worst dogs to own. The irresponsible APBT/Amstaff owner could have a dog that could be as bad as any other breed of large or strong, potentially aggressive dogs in a similarly undisciplined situation!

The UKC Standard for the American Pit Bull Terrier (APBT)

Head: The head should be medium length and bricklike in shape. The skull is flat and widest at the ears, with prominent cheeks free from wrinkles.

Muzzle: The muzzle is square, wide, and deep. Well-pronounced jaws should display strength. The upper teeth should meet tightly over the lower teeth, outside in front.

Ears: The ears are cropped or uncropped (not important) and should be set high on the head, free from wrinkles.

Eyes: The round eyes should be set far apart, low down on the skull. Any color is acceptable.

Nose: The nose should have wide open nostrils. Any color is acceptable.

Neck: The neck is muscular and slightly arched. It should taper from shoulder to head, free from looseness of skin.

Shoulders: The shoulders should be strong and muscular, with wide sloping shoulder blades.

Back: Although short and strong, the back should slightly slope from the withers to the rump. It should be slightly arched at the loins, which should be slightly tucked.

Chest: The chest should be deep, but not too broad, with wide sprung ribs.

Ribs: The close ribs should be well sprung, with deep back ribs.

Tail: Although short in comparison to size, the tail should be set low and taper to a fine point. It should not be carried over the back. A bobbed tail is not acceptable.

Legs: The legs should be large and round boned, with straight, upright pasterns, and be reasonably strong. The feet should be of medium size. The gait should be light and springy, with no rolling or pacing.

Thigh: The thigh should be long with muscles developed and hocks down straight.

Coat: The coat should be glossy and be short and stiff to the touch.

Color: Any color or markings are permissible.

Weight: The weight is not important. The preferred weight for females is from 30 to 50 pounds (13.6–22.7 kg); for males, from 35 to 60 pounds (15.9–27.2 kg).

The AKC Standard for the American Staffordshire Terrier (Amstaff)

General Impression: The American Staffordshire Terrier should give the impression of great strength for its size. It should be put together well, be muscular but agile and graceful, and be keenly alive to its surroundings. It should be

The American Pit Bull Terrier/American Staffordshire Terrier is a medium-sized dog with an impressive physique and demeanor.

stocky, not long legged or racy in outline. Its courage is proverbial.

Head: The head should be medium length, deep through, with a broad skull, very pronounced cheek muscles, and a distinct stop; and the ears should be set high.

Ears: The ears should be cropped or uncropped, the latter preferred. Uncropped ears should be short and held half rose or prick. A full drop is to be penalized.

Eyes: The eyes should be dark and round, laid down in the skull and set far apart. No pink eyelids.

Muzzle: Although medium length, the muzzle should be rounded on the upper side to fall away abruptly below the eyes. The jaws are well defined. The underjaw is to be strong and have biting power. The lips are close and even, with no looseness. The upper teeth are to meet tightly outside the lower teeth in front. The nose is definitely black.

Neck: The neck should be heavy, slightly arched, tapering from the shoulders to the back of the skull, with no looseness of skin and be medium in length.

Shoulders: The shoulders should be strong and muscular, with blades wide and sloping.

Back: The back should be fairly short and have a slight sloping from the withers to the rump, with a gentle short slope at the rump to the base of the tail. The loins should be slightly tucked.

Body: The body should have well-sprung ribs, deep in the rear. All ribs should be close together. The forelegs should be set rather wide apart to permit chest development. The chest should be deep and round.

Tail: Although short in comparison to size, the tail should be low set, tapering to a fine point, not curled or held over the back. The tail is not docked.

Legs: The front legs should be straight, with large or round bones, and pastern upright. No resemblance of a bend in the front should exist. The hindquarters should be well muscled, let down at the hocks, turning neither in nor out. The feet should be of moderate size, well arched, and compact. The gait must be springy without roll or pace.

Coat: The coat should be short, close, stiff to the touch, and glossy.

Color: Any color—solid, parti, or patched—is permissible. However, all-white, more than 80 percent white, black and tan, and liver are not to be encouraged.

Size: The height and weight should be in proportion. A height of about 18 to 19 inches (45.7–48.3 cm) at the shoulders for the male and 17 to 18 inches (43.2–45.7 cm) for the female is considered preferable.

Faults: Faults to be penalized are Dudley nose, light or pink eyes, tail too long or badly carried, and undershot or overshot mouth.

HISTORY OF THE APBT/AMSTAFF

The American Pit Bull Terrier and the American Staffordshire Terrier along with the Staffordshire Bull Terrier and the white and colored varieties of the (long-faced) Bull Terrier all share much the same genetic heritage. Whether or not modern breeders want to acknowledge it, this common heritage is deeply rooted in what has been called the blood sports. The APBT, the Amstaff, and the others all spring from a canine ancestry that fought other animals: bulls, bears, other dogs, and even lions!

To refuse to face the historical truth, as distasteful and barbaric as it may be, is to fail to grasp the source of many of the qualities that have caused these breeds not only to endure but to flourish. To understand the positive traits about the modern dogs, one must understand the negative things that caused them.

The Bulldog

The Bulldog part of the APBT and Amstaff equation was not the squat, lumbering, quite short-faced bulldog of today. The bulldog of several centuries ago was an agile, muscular dog of medium size, quite capable of participating in the bull-baiting and bear-baiting events of the time. Bulldogs were admired for their tenacity,

Familiarity with the history of the APBT/Amstaff is crucial to understanding today's dog.

their physical courage (gameness), and their tolerance of pain—all good attributes for dogs battling foes many times their size.

Artists' renderings of the bulldog of the eighteenth and nineteenth centuries show an animal strikingly similar to the American Staffordshire Terrier and the American Pit Bull Terrier of today. This similarity of appearance has led many "fighting pit bull" authorities to claim that the modern APBTs have *no* terrier blood at all! In books and descriptions by some of these authorities, the American Pit Bull Terrier is often simply referred to as a bulldog. These sources sometimes put forth the belief that the American Pit Bull Terrier is, in reality, merely the original bulldog of the British Isles!

Other historical records do not support this claim. Numerous references cite intentional crosses between bulldogs and terriers. The reason for this mixing of two varieties was to increase the speed and activity levels of the bulldog by genetically adding attributes of the agile and active hunting terriers of the time.

The early British Bulldogs were not crossbred exclusively with terriers. So admired was the physical toughness of the bulldog that a famous bulldog cross was made with racing Greyhounds in an attempt to instill toughness in a very dissimilar breed. Another mixing of bulldog lines led to a new breed. In an attempt to develop a more suitable patrol dog for English gamekeepers, the early bulldog was bred to the huge English Mastiff. The result was the Bull Mastiff, a tough, agile, quick dog of still considerable size.

Bull and bear fighting in England was outlawed by the Humane Acts of Parliament in 1835. Dog fighting, while not new, became more popular. This occurred partly because of the edict against the larger animal fights and partly because dog fights could be staged in secret much more easily. The bulldog, so ideally suited for bedeviling bulls and bears, was a bit too slow and too methodical for the dog fighters. More speed and flair were needed to bring gambling spectators to the clandestine fights. Hunting terriers of the time not only possessed an inbred desire to fight other animals, but they had grit and courage of their own to bring to the mixture. The crossing of the tenacious bulldog and the aggressive terrier became more and more commonplace as the demand for dogs to fight dogs increased.

The Terrier

Terriers had long been used for hunting and then attacking many types of animals. Fox Terriers accompanied foxhound packs to enter dens and kill or drive out the inhabitants. Terriers were also used against badgers, otters, and other creatures. Terriers excelled in killing. Their speed and apparent desire to kill rats made them useful in a time when rodents were a major blight.

Some sources state that the bull-and-terrier breeds resulted from interbreeding of the now-extinct white English Terrier (which resembled the shape and size of the Manchester Terrier). Other authorities assert that any of several types of the larger hunting terriers were crossed

with bulldogs. To support this latter position, they point out that some bull-and-terrier breeds had wiry coats and a variety of colors not found in bulldogs or in the white English Terriers.

The Bull-and-Terrier Breeds

The APBT, the Staffordshire Bull Terrier, and the Amstaff are certainly breeds that fall into the bull-and-terrier classification (the pure bulldog crowd notwithstanding). However, they are not the only ones that qualify as bull-and-terrier breeds.

Dog breeders had always been willing to go outside a particular breed type to gain some attribute or quality. James Hinks developed what would become the immensely popular white Bull Terrier with its long, Roman-nosed face. Hinks not only used bulldog and white English Terrier bloodlines but reportedly blended in the Dalmatian and possibly the Spanish Pointer to produce an all-white breed. The early Staffordshire Terrier was next crossed into Hinks's all-white breed to produce the colored Bull Terrier variety. Other than the long, down face, the Bull Terriers, both white and colored, have a similar physique to that of the APBT and the Amstaff.

The small, dapper Boston Terrier, which has been classified by the American Kennel Club in its Non-Sporting Group, is also a bull-and-terrier breed. Although its house pet status is far from the image of the other bulldog/terrier types, the Boston's heritage contains many of the same forebears of the APBT and the Amstaff. The now-extinct white English Terrier that played such a key role in the development of so many bull-and-terrier breeds, and other terrier breeds as well, was also a part of the Boston's makeup along with small bulldogs.

The Staffordshire Bull Terrier (nicknamed the Stafford or Staffybull) is a solid bull-and-terrier breed that almost got lost in the American Pit Bull and American Staffordshire notoriety. Although recognized by the Kennel Club of England in 1936 and the American Kennel Club in 1978, the Stafford is thought to be the oldest of the bull-and-terrier breeds. The working-class people of Staffordshire, in central England, had long enjoyed the blood sports, and the area was recognized for its fighting dogs. Many of these dogs found their way from Staffordshire to America. These dogs then played a key part in the development of the American Pit Bull Terrier and the American Staffordshire Terrier.

Today's Staffybull is shorter and smaller than either the Amstaff or the APBT. Its ears are always left uncropped (uncut). Currently the most popular terrier in Britain, the Stafford has gained friends the world over for its good disposition, confident style, and devotion to its owners.

The Fighters

Depending on whom you ask, dog fighters are either cruel monsters who have created canine Frankensteins that should be expunged from the dog world or are dedicated, persecuted sports lovers who have kept alive their dogs' natural abilities to do what the dogs love to do. Either of these positions represents an opposite view that leaves the APBT and (to a

lesser but still certain degree) the Amstaff squarely in the middle.

Dog fighting has been illegal for over a hundred years. Yet, to assume that dog fighting no longer exists would be naive. Even though pit fights still take place, the average person would probably have difficulty finding one. State and federal laws in the United States have forced whatever dog fighting remains to be a secretive, clandestine activity. Even writers whose works contain a lot of information about this illicit activity are probably outside the core group of die-hard dog fighters who still survive.

Like cock fighters, dog fighters were always a clannish crowd whose breeding, conditioning, and training techniques were closely held secrets. It is interesting to note that as repulsive as most people find dog fighting, the dog fighters were among the first to keep careful records about pedigrees. What has become commonplace for all registered, purebred dog

These two exemplify the difference between cropped ears (front) and uncropped (rear).

Above: Both Amstaffs and APBTs are used in work with cattle and other livestock, as this blue brindle female is doing with this calf.

Left: Like puppies of any breed, APBT/Amstaff pups need a lot of attention.

breeders today was originally widely practiced many decades ago by the breeders of fighting dogs.

England, Scotland, Ireland, and the United States brought the bull-and-terrier breeds to their ultimate fighting form. Each country had its own variety of fighter. England had its Staffordshire Bulls. Scotland produced the Blue Paul (or Blue Poll)—a large, usually slate gray battler. Ireland exported to America many of the small, red-colored, red-eyed, and red-nosed bull-and-terrier breeds that would become known as the Old Family Red Nose line. The pit bulls and Amstaffs of the United States not only descended from the fighting dogs of the British

Above: Dogs of this breed tend to have very wide, muscular necks.

Top right: The APBT and Amstaff come in many colors and patterns. This fawn-and-white dog is just one example.

Bottom right: These two animals are content to be just house dogs.

Isles but spread the bull-and-terrier dogs over a much larger landscape.

Contrary to popular misconception, the pit-fighting dogs are not generally the vicious beasts that are responsible for attacks on humans. A recent news program on television showed a dog fight filmed by a hidden camera. Although gruesome to watch, at the end of set periods of time, the dog handlers were allowed to pick up and administer some rudimentary care to their fighters.

Uncontrollable, vicious dogs would have been impossible to treat in this manner. Any-

The original British Bulldog was bred for bear-baiting and other "blood sports." This early bulldog greatly resembled today's American Pit Bull Terrier or American Staffordshire Terrier.

dogs that produce puppies that are readily available to the average person. A person will find a true fighting strain dog for sale in the classified ads of a newspaper just about as often as one would find a true racing Greyhound, a true Alaskan Iditarod quality sled dog, or a surefire AKC dog show winner.

one who has ever tried to help an injured dog knows the possibility of getting bitten. The dogs in this fight were obviously of the bull-and-terrier sort. They were also in the heat of battle and probably in some pain. However, the dogs did not attack their handlers when taken to their respective corners for a rest.

Additionally, pit dogs are a very valuable commodity to the microsegment of the population that advocates dog fighting. These dogs are not allowed to roam the streets. They are not usually indiscriminately bred to the kind of

Finding the Right Name

Breed names have often been devices of political convenience. The American Pit Bull Terrier has been known as the half-and-half (probably referring to its crossbred heritage), the American Bull Terrier, the Yankee Terrier, and others. As stated, many dog fight proponents referred to and continue to refer to the breed just as a Bull Dog. The name American Pit Bull Terrier was chosen by an American, C. Z. Bennett, in 1898. Bennett, founder of the United Kennel Club (UKC), not only gave the breed its name but developed the official rules regulating dog pits and dog fighting. The UKC became the official registry for the American Pit Bull Terrier.

Note: Although the UKC did support and regulate dog fighting in the early 1900s, the current organization strongly disavows any support of dog fighting activities and will expel any members suspected of even advertising dogs or anything else having to do with fighting. The UKC is still the primary APBT (under that name) registry, but the organization now

Three Canine Heroes

Corporal Dog, an American Pit Bull Terrier, has served as the official canine mascot of the United States Marine Corps for many years. Another APBT named Stubby was the most decorated American war dog in World War I. And more recently, an APBT was officially designated a hero for repeatedly rescuing people and livestock during the 1993 floods in the Midwest.

also maintains records on over 200 other breeds as well!

The American Kennel Club (AKC) repeatedly rejected the American Pit Bull Terrier for admission. The AKC was stringent in its refusal to accept a breed tainted by the word *pit* and the fighting dog sanctioning espoused by the UKC at the time. Not until the APBT breeders agreed to a word game did the AKC go along and grant recognition *not* to the American Pit Bull Terrier but to the Staffordshire Terrier! The American Dog Breeders Association is an organization formed exclusively for the American Pit Bull Terrier. The ADBA holds shows and other events for the APBTs and registers only dogs of this breed. The gameness and physical aspects of the American Pit Bull Terrier are outlined at length in the ADBA. If a person is interested only in the working game-bred APBT, the ADBA is the organization to contact; see "Information," page 108.

There was some support for several names such as the American Bull Terrier. The white and colored Bull Terrier breeders (Hinks's creation) rankled at this, and the Staffordshire name was chosen as a compromise. By changing the name of the APBTs they wanted included in the AKC, the breeders of the newly named dogs got official AKC acceptance in 1936.

The name game was not over yet. In 1974, the Kennel Club of England's Staffordshire Bull Terrier was admitted to the American Kennel Club, which already had its version of the

A Tough Act to Follow

Several APBT/Amstaffs, such as Petey of *The Little Rascals* fame, have become accomplished canine actors. Dog trainers for film and television rank these breeds among the easiest to train, and they sure seem to have great screen presence!

APBT—the Staffordshire Terrier. To try to prevent any more misunderstandings, the AKC supported one more name change and created the American Staffordshire Terrier. Both the Amstaff and the Staffybull are well-received members of the AKC today.

An interesting sleight of name opportunity has occurred because the two largest dog registries in the United States recognize the dogs of essentially the same breeds by different names. A number of UKC-registered American Pit Bull Terriers are also AKC-registered American Staffordshire Terriers! These double-registered dogs can compete in dog shows or obedience events in either organization. Recently a dog with dual registration won top honors in both the AKC and the UKC!

Some APBTs are registered with only the UKC and some Amstaffs are in only the AKC. These must be shown only within their respective organizations. Their offspring will also be allowed only the registry of their parents. A dog that is dual or double registered must be born to parents that are both double registered.

SHOULD YOU OWN AN APBT/AMSTAFF?

Purchasing any breed of dog is a big responsibility, but the APBT/Amstaff has special needs. A prospective owner needs to familiarize him/herself with the responsibilities that come with caring for one of these breeds.

Basic Dog Owner Responsibilities

Every owner of any breed or type of dog should be responsible, aware, and caring. The need for proper housing, medical care, food, training, and socialization are just some of the basic requirements that should be understood before any person undertakes owning any dog.

Unless a potential dog owner is willing and able to give these essentials, dog ownership should be delayed or even avoided altogether. To own a pet and to not provide for its needs is certainly cruel, neglectful, and even illegal.

Responsibilities Specific to APBT/Amstaff Owners

Because of controversy that surrounds the APBT, American Staffordshire Terrier, and similar dogs, potential owners of these dogs must be even more aware of their responsibilities

Both APBTs and Amstaffs are dogs of great dignity, great strength, and a great need for just the right owner.

than owners of many other breeds. The owner of an American Pit Bull Terrier or an Amstaff will need:

✔ An aware, alert approach to APBT/Amstaff ownership, recognizing the need for the best-quality dog from the best-quality background.

✔ An understanding that not everyone will welcome the presence of an Amstaff or an APBT into a neighborhood, into a city park, or even onto a public street accompanied by its owner!

✔ Adequate fencing, adequate housing, adequate training, and positive attitudes about protecting an APBT or an Amstaff from becoming lost, strayed, or involved in something that could bring harm.

✔ Previous personal experience with other kinds of dogs combined with a high degree of acquired knowledge about Amstaffs and APBTs.

✔ An understanding and protective attitude by all members of an APBT's or an Amstaff's household that the pet's control and safety should always be a prime consideration.

Should an APBT/Amstaff Be Your First Dog?

In a word, no. Most people who know and love these breeds believe that the APBT/Amstaff should not be a first-time owner's dog. This does not mean that there are not some wonderful Amstaffs or American Pit Bull Terriers that could be great first dogs, but these special dogs need special owners, and rarely is a first-time dog owner ready.

The physical attributes of these breeds and the negative public attitude that sometimes follows them may be more than a novice dog owner will be able to handle. The well-bred, well-trained, and well-cared-for APBT or American Staffordshire in the hands of the well-prepared owner can be the equal of any other breed. However, the emphasis has to be on the well-prepared owner.

Male or Female?

In some breeds, the gender of the pet is a relatively minor concern. In the hands of an experienced dog owner thoroughly familiar with the Amstaff or the American Pit Bull Terrier, whether a pet is a male or a female is probably purely a matter of personal preference. For a first-time Amstaff or APBT owner, many breeders recommend a female.

A female of any breed is generally a little less challenging for pet owners. Male dogs of most breeds tend to be more aggressive, not that females cannot be aggressive. Unneutered males will arduously pursue females in heat. In a neighborhood, this could lead to several kinds of negative consequences.

Discuss your personal preferences with several knowledgeable American Staffordshire Terrier or American Pit Bull Terrier breeders. Get them to assess your current situation as a potential dog owner. Weigh their advice along with what you believe is a wise course of action in gender selection. Combine this with the choice that makes the most common sense.

Puppy or Older Dog?

Some very excellent adult dogs may be available to you. If you have the experience and capacity to help an older Amstaff or APBT adjust to a new home and family, you could consider this option. However, as with a preference for males or females, a number of breeders suggest that if you have never owned an Amstaff or an American Pit Bull Terrier before, a puppy is the better choice.

An American Pit Bull Terrier or an American Staffordshire Terrier puppy will give you ample opportunity to mold it and shape it into the best pet its genetic makeup will allow it to be. Unlike an adult, this youngster will not have a lengthy past history (positive or negative) to forget. You can concentrate on initial training and socialization rather than on retraining and resocialization.

An American Staffordshire or American Pit Bull Terrier puppy will have an opportunity to grow up as one of the family. When a family is well prepared for the addition of a puppy, the

A puppy will grow up with you and become what you make of it.

CHECKLIST

Is the APBT/Amstaff Right for You?

There are some key points to consider about owning an APBT or an Amstaff.

✔ These breeds have been shrouded by a lot of misinformation and controversy.

✔ Not everyone in your neighborhood, in your circle of friends, in a city park, or even on a public street will welcome your ownership of one of these dogs.

✔ Some communities have placed breed-specific restrictions against dogs like the APBT and the Amstaff.

✔ Some insurance companies will not issue homeowner's policies for the owners of dogs of certain breeds.

✔ Dogs of these two breeds should have stronger fencing, housing, training, and other controls than dogs of some other breeds.

✔ American Pit Bull Terriers come from animal-aggressive ancestry and will require significantly more owner attention involving effective training and socialization.

✔ Pound for pound, these dogs are the strongest canines in the world. Some chew toys sufficient for almost every other breed are insufficient for the APBT and the Amstaff.

✔ Amstaffs and APBTs tend to be smart, alert dogs that will need early, consistent training.

✔ These breeds have been exploited for generations by people whose idea of dog ownership differs radically from most pet owners.

APBTs have unfortunately become popular with street toughs and with some unsavory elements in society.

✔ The popularity and name recognition afforded these breeds has caused a great deal of ill-advised breeding that has become a self-fulfilling prophecy.

✔ In the hands of the right owners, the right American Staffordshire Terrier or the right American Pit Bull Terrier can be a family pet of legendary proportions, the kind that you tell your grandchildren about!

✔ In the hands of the wrong owners, the wrong American Staffordshire Terrier or the wrong American Pit Bull Terrier can become at best an unfortunate mistake, at worst a serious mistake that will negatively impact on the owners and the dog.

✔ Because these breeds stem from dogs of pit-fighting infamy, even a slight nip or a scratch from a dog's toenail can result in legal action and/or legal consequences that probably would not happen if the nipper or scratcher were some other breed.

✔ The APBT and the Amstaff will need close human interaction—living with the family and being a part of the family—to reach its ultimate potential as a pet and companion.

✔ These dogs cannot be tied to a tree or simply left in a kennel or backyard. They are true lovers of people and will suffer if deprived of lots of human contact.

youngster can easily become an integral part of everyday activity. When a puppy is brought into an unprepared or ill-prepared household, the chances for a less-than-satisfactory outcome are greatly increased.

Pet Quality or Show Quality?

The accent in any breed of dog should always be on quality of the animal's health and temperament first, then on show or pet considerations. Your goals for your Amstaff or APBT will play an important role in whether you want a potential show dog or can settle for a top-dispositioned, healthy animal with some minor cosmetic flaw that stops a conformation dog show career.

Many opportunities are available to show both APBTs and Amstaffs. The people involved

The decision to involve your pet in dog shows is a matter of personal choice, but your first responsibility to a dog is toward its health and well-being.

APBT owners should expect some prejudice from fellow dog owners, due to misconceptions about the breed.

in dog showing generally greatly enjoy it. This may or may not be the activity of choice for you and your dog. However, dog shows are often a good place to start gaining breed knowledge. Dog shows and obedience events can often be the right place to start getting a list of breeders from whom a puppy could be purchased.

APBT or Amstaff?

Whether to own an American Staffordshire Terrier or an American Pit Bull Terrier is purely a matter of personal choice. Some breeders of these dogs consider them much the same breed with the main distinction being that of registries, not dogs. In the past, the *pit* part of the APBT name was enough to discourage some people from owning one. Some of these people turned to the American Staffordshire, which had been bred along AKC exhibition lines. You can find an Amstaff breeder (or an APBT breeder) near you by contacting the national clubs (see "Information," page 108).

Although the Amstaff is still a good choice, the APBT of the UKC now also has a bright future in the showring as more and more UKC (and other organizations accepting the APBT) shows are held. Although not everyone is interested in dog shows and dog showing, show breeders are often the source for some top-quality pet pups.

Children and puppies brought up together can become the very best of friends.

Of course, a large number of dual or double-registered Amstaff/APBTs are still available that can compete in either UKC or AKC shows! Dogs of legitimate double-registered status are neither better nor worse than their single-registered kin. However, they do offer opportunities in both the major kennel clubs.

Regardless of which breed you choose, you and your family will need to consider some important facts carefully. The next section discusses these. Of course, any dog will need and deserve good care, affection, and the attention of a knowledgeable owner.

Are You Ready for an APBT/Amstaff?

Before you go out and get an APBT or an Amstaff, you should ask yourself the following questions and then answer them honestly:

✔ Do you want an APBT/Amstaff just to have the reputation for owning the meanest dog on the block?

✔ Have you owned other kinds of dogs that will give you some reference point and some experience for owning an APBT or an Amstaff?

✔ Are you willing to invest the time and money to search for and find just the right pet for you and your family?

✔ Do you have the resources and the inclination to help a young puppy get the socialization, care, and training it will need to grow into the best-possible pet?

✔ Do you and your family have the time and space to share with a dog that will need a lot of affection, direction, and attention?

✔ Are you aware of the negative publicity that has attached itself to these dogs, and are you ready to deal with any negative spillover that

may affect you when you own an Amstaff or an APBT?

✔ Are you willing to go the extra dog-owner mile for a dog that may need more than other dogs do but would willingly die for its family?

✔ Are you willing to spay or neuter an obvious pet specimen?

✔ Will you do everything within your power to keep any dog that you own from becoming a public nuisance, a threat to itself or others, or one of the millions of animal shelter dogs euthanized each year?

These are tough questions that any serious, prospective APBT or Amstaff owner should be able to answer. If you or your family stumble over some of these or if an answer does not seem to serve the best interests of the potential pet, your path is clearer than you may think. Potential pet owners who have trouble with these questions have several options:

1. Consider another kind of dog. The APBT/Amstaff may not be right for you and your lifestyle.

2. Do not get any dog at all. Pet ownership requires a great deal of responsibility, regardless of what breed you choose.

3. Postpone getting a dog until you are better able to afford the time, money, and other expenditures that an APBT/Amstaff will require.

4. Find a responsible American Pit Bull Terrier or American Staffordshire Terrier breeder to visit, to spend time with, and to question.

Pluses to Balance the Negatives

Having to consider these negatives and to review your own dog-owning motivation may seem to cast American Staffordshires and American Pit Bull Terriers into a bad light. Saying that one of these dogs just is not worth the

CHECKLIST

The Right Preparation

Before you seriously get down to choosing the right puppy, you should do the following things:

✔ Read everything available about these breeds.

✔ Talk with as many reputable Amstaff or APBT breeders as possible.

✔ Visit a number of dog shows, obedience events, and kennels to see these dogs up close.

✔ Talk to other dog experts, perhaps local veterinarians, dog trainers, and breeders of other breeds, to get their assessment of a particular kennel or of APBT/Amstaffs in general.

✔ Look at your current life situation as to how it would fit the needs of a fast-growing, inquisitive, new puppy.

✔ With tact, review your insurance policies and coverage. (One top Amstaff breeder suggests that you quietly increase your homeowner's insurance to the $300,000 level *prior* to purchasing a puppy.)

✔ Check the laws within your township, parish, county, or city to see if they have any breed-specific laws banning certain dogs.

✔ Decide exactly what you think you want, an Amstaff or an APBT (or both in a double-registered animal), a male or a female, a puppy or an older dog, a purely pet prospect or a show/pet prospect. You can discuss color preferences and other more cosmetic aspects while remembering that good health and a good disposition are the key elements that you really want.

✔ Seek a mentor or several mentors who are experienced APBT or Amstaff breeders. They should help you not only with your search for the right pet but should be around to share advice and assistance as you and your puppy grow up together.

extra effort would be easy, but that would not be true.

The best dog-owning family in the world who buys a puppy on impulse or a puppy that comes from poorly bred stock with behavioral and health problems will almost certainly come to regret it. The best APBT or Amstaff puppy in the world coming into a neglectful, careless, ill-prepared family is a recipe for trouble.

Responsible, careful owners of these dogs tell wonderful stories that would do any breed proud. These stories are not only of the incredible bravery and devotion one would naturally expect of such dogs. Some accounts point out the animals' sensitive nature. Others show a brightness that would make the fictional Lassie envious. Still further stories illustrate the whimsical, funny aspects of these powerful animals.

The APBT and the Amstaff have been vigorously vilified. Even after all the bad press, these dogs have thousands upon thousands of fans who know the actual and the potential of the APBT and Amstaff and who cherish them!

CONSIDERATIONS BEFORE BUYING

The Right Attitude

Before you begin your quest for just the right Amstaff or APBT you should adopt a particular mind-set. It may be true that Michelangelo formed one of his greatest sculptures from a flawed piece of stone, but there was only one Michelangelo. For you to have the best-possible outcome with your Amstaff or American Pit Bull Terrier, you should start with the best-possible puppy. Then sculpt and mold it by good socialization, good care, and effective training.

What You Should Expect

Most reputable Amstaff and APBT breeders will be as concerned about whether you should get one of their puppies as you are. This concern, often reflected by the breeder asking you a number of questions, is a good sign that this breeder really cares about finding loving, life-long homes for all puppies produced.

You should expect to pay a fair price, generally $300 to $500, for a healthy pet prospect from stock with good temperaments. Healthy, well-dispositioned show prospects will cost you more, depending on breeder and location. Beware of bargains. With Amstaffs and APBTs, you positively cannot afford them. Bargain

Don't even consider an APBT/Amstaff as a pet unless you know you'll have ample time to spend with your new friend.

puppies often become much more expensive than many top show dogs would be!

Popularity has its perils. Especially for American Pit Bull Terriers, one can see many classified ads offering puppies in the Sunday newspapers in every major city. Some of these litters may possibly be from healthy dogs with excellent temperaments. More likely, these ads reflect a casual mating of two dogs that should have never been bred. You have a better chance finding buried treasure or striking oil in your own backyard than in getting just the puppy you want in this manner.

Remember that this little puppy will grow to be a powerful adult and that you are going to be making not only the puppy but its adult version a member of your household. Go for the best and ignore the rest! Before choosing an American Staffordshire or American Pit Bull Terrier from any breeder, you should be certain that the puppy of your choice has several vital documents:

Health records: This will be the pup's medical history showing the dates of all veterinarian examinations, wormings, vaccinations, and any treatments the pup may have had and for what.

The AKC or UKC registration papers: These forms, from their respective kennel clubs, affirm that this Amstaff or APBT puppy is a purebred (its mother and father were purebreds and registered). You should also get applications that you can send to the AKC or UKC (or both if the pup's parents were both dual registered) to register your puppy in your name.

Canine hip dysplasia (CHD) screening: You will want test results pertaining to the parents of your puppy and their examinations for canine hip dysplasia (CHD) (see page 95). Although these results are not a guarantee that your pup will be free from this ailment, CHD screening is the only predictive testing that may be currently available to you. OFA (Orthopedic Foundation for Animals) or CHD testing is performed for potential breeders when the stud dog or bitch is two years old.

Note: The Penn hip testing (which can be done by only specially trained veterinary practitioners) and some other forms of prescreening can be done on younger animals. You would be wise to use whatever testing is available to you to ascertain the hip health of your APBT or Amstaff.

A rule concerning documents: Before you become too attached to a puppy, make sure that the dog's papers are available to you. Quite simply, if they are not available, do not buy the puppy! Most reputable breeders are honest and are not out to cheat you. However, you want to avoid what could be called the "puppy buyer's lament" which is "The breeder said the papers are in the mail!"

Guarantees

All responsible Amstaff and APBT breeders will give you a reasonable and written health and temperament guarantee about any puppy you buy from them. This should state that the dog's inherited health and temperament are guaranteed. If an inherited problem occurs, you can return the puppy. Confident breeders who have taken real care in choosing the ancestry of their dogs usually know from the breeding that a properly handled puppy will be healthy and have a good disposition.

You are not the only party in this agreement that will want a guarantee. Responsible dog breeders often ask for several written assurances from you regarding a puppy from their kennel. One of these involves the spaying or neutering of a pet-quality dog or puppy. This is done to insure that only the very best specimens are slated for the breeding pen. A spay/neuter agreement does not imply that your puppy is not a good, healthy animal. It means only that the cosmetic flaw that keeps your pet from being a show dog should also keep it from being a breeding dog. The only exception to the documents rule is that some breeders will hold registration papers until they receive proof that a veterinarian has spayed or neutered a pet puppy. Some breeders who sell show quality puppies will want a guarantee from you that the show prospect will be shown and given a chance to go as far toward a conformation championship as possible.

Many reputable breeders have a return policy where they will want your puppy back if you find you cannot keep it. This strong proprietary interest in the future of a puppy is one of the best signs that you have chosen a quality breeder. Responsible breeders do not want their puppies to end up chained to the bumper of a wrecked car in a junkyard, given to the mysterious friend in the country, or sent to almost certain death at an animal shelter.

Selecting the Right Puppy

Suppose that you and your family have decided that you would like to have a female

American Staffordshire from parentage that has done well in obedience work. After looking at the rainbow of canine colors that Amstaffs come in, you like the crisp look of black with a white ring around its neck. Your secondary color choice (always a good idea) is slate blue with the white markings, with brindle and white being a third choice. Because you do not anticipate showing or breeding, you have elected to purchase a bright, healthy, sweet-natured pet prospect and will have her spayed when she is old enough.

Because you have taken time to concentrate on the traits you would like to have in your new pet, you have a better chance of avoiding first-puppy syndrome. All Amstaff puppies tend to be adorable. An impulsive person or family can undo all the long hours of study and research by falling in love with the first puppy or with the first litter seen. That first pup may indeed be the best for you, but it will still be the best after you have looked at as many puppies as possible.

When you have found an Amstaff litter that has the prerequisite obedience work heritage that you want and has several female pet-quality puppies with white collars, you should now see which puppy seems well adjusted within the litter. You may not want the most aggressive. However, neither will you want the shrinking violet that avoids your touch.

A good breeder will have already begun the crucial socialization process with this litter. The puppies should be at ease and even curious and

happy to see strangers. Their mother should be alert but not threatened by your presence. If you can see the puppies' sire (father), approach him, and pet him, you may be about to buy a puppy.

Before You Bring Your Puppy Home

Well before the time that you enter your home with your new Amstaff or American Pit Bull Terrier puppy, you must do many things to get ready. Because your puppy will need to live in the house with you, you will need to make the home safe for the inquisitive, chewing youngster. You will need to work out your plan to house-break the puppy. You will need to make some necessary purchases. You will want to assess each area to which the puppy will have access for things that might harm the youngster.

Essential Purchases

The first essential purchase and one of the most important is to buy some of the exact same food the breeder has been feeding your new puppy, unless the breeder has been having

Essential purchases for a new puppy include a crate or carrier, food and water dishes, a grooming brush and comb, a toenail clipper, and some really tough toys and treats.

trouble with this particular food. You can change diets, if you absolutely must, at some later date. Do not change a new puppy's food. Doing so can only add to the trauma the youngster is already experiencing!

Because your Amstaff or APBT should live indoors with you, the next purchase that is also of great importance is a dog cage/crate/carrier that will serve as your pup's home within your home. (See "Crate Training," page 75).

Your new family member will need its own water and food bowls. Remember the powerful jaws of these dogs, and get dishes made of strong metal or ceramic material. Get a sturdy, flat-bottomed design that is large enough for permanent use and that will not be easily tipped over.

By using your breeder/mentor's experience, get a leash (also called a lead) with an appropri-

ately sized collar for your puppy. This will be the pup's regular collar. Because training begins early with APBTs and American Staffordshires, you will also need a training collar.

Ask your breeder friend about the right brush for the pup's short, smooth coat. Like most things with Amstaffs and APBTs, the earlier you start something, the easier it will be. Even though these dogs shed very little and require little grooming, you will want to get the pup accustomed to the brush while it is still very young for those times when brushing is needed.

Another essential early purchase is your puppy's own toothbrush. By initiating teeth cleaning while the puppy is still small, brushing the dog's teeth will not be a problem when the dog is older (and stronger).

Toys for the American Staffordshire Terrier and the American Pit Bull Terrier differ from those for almost any other breed. The jaw strength of these dogs, even as puppies, can reduce even tough-looking chew toys into rubble in a surprisingly short time. These dogs have a great potential for intestinal blockage because they swallow pieces of what seemed to be indestructible toys. Ask your experienced breed mentor for recommendations about the best chew items for your Amstaff/APBT.

Housing, Inside and Out

With few exceptions, American Pit Bull Terriers and American Staffordshire Terriers should live inside your home with you. Their short coats and unusually thin layer of body fat generally call for housing your pet inside.

The APBT/Amstaff's coat is short and smooth, but your pet will still need the occasional brushing.

Puppies are cute, but they are also very malleable. They will become what they are bred, socialized, and trained to be.

So cold-sensitive are some APBTs and Amstaffs that one breeder told of her five house dogs (all females) following the rays of the sun as they moved from room to room during the passing of the day. These dogs (all dual registered) would actually jockey for the warmest spot when they migrated with the sun!

If you will occasionally use outside housing in warmer climes or seasons, forget the old drums and logging chains. Instead, invest in an insulated and draft-proof doghouse and place it within a secure fenced yard or kennel run.

Certainly the best reason for sharing your home with your new pet is that it desperately needs your companionship and supervision. Human interaction or the lack thereof is responsible for some of the misbehavior that can be legitimately pinned on purebred APBTs or Amstaffs.

The Cage/Crate/Carrier

Your Amstaff/APBT is, like the wolf and coyote, a denning animal. In the wild, dogs will have a den of some sort most of their lives. Even if your pet lives inside with you, it needs a place of its own.

Various models are available on the market. They range from the plastic airline-type carriers to cages to crates. Because cages and crates have metal construction—remember the jaw power of these breeds—these are the models most suggested.

The cage or crate is not only a humane way to keep your pet where you want it to be at times, it also makes use of the denning instinct.

The crate-training concept is also a wonderful aid in housebreaking (see "Housebreaking," page 73) and in giving your new pup its first place to sleep.

The Fenced Yard

If you and your family are fortunate enough to live where you can have a fenced backyard, this will be a real benefit for your APBT/Amstaff puppy. You will be able to give the youngster longer outside breaks than you may be able to on walks.

Some factors are important about fencing for APBTs and Amstaffs. These dogs are great climbers and great diggers! They can make short work of flimsy wooden fencing and have been known to stretch lighter-gauge fencing fabric.

If you have the option, make your fence strong, high, and tunnel resistant. If you cannot do this, do not leave your dog unattended in the backyard!

HOW-TO: PUPPY PROOFING

Making your home and area safe for your new APBT or Amstaff puppy is a little different than it would be for a puppy of most other breeds. The jaws of even an APBT or Amstaff puppy are very, very strong. Things that would get only a little gnawing from a puppy of another breed will practically disintegrate when chewed by a little APBT or American Staffordshire. You may have raised other pups, but this one is different.

You will want to decide just where the pup will be allowed to go. Not every part of any home is a good place for a curiosity-filled little terrier. Talk with your breeder-mentor about additional places that should be off-limits for a new puppy and why. Here are some ways to accomplish this very important task:

When puppy proofing your home, get down to the puppy's level to look for possible dangers.

Puppy proofing includes protecting a teething puppy from almost certain death by chewing electric cords.

✔ Get down to the puppy's level, and look for things or situations where a little dog could get hurt. This is a great, fun, and instructive chore where children could help.

✔ Look for electric cords, low-sitting houseplants, doorstops, and other everyday items that might harm a chewing puppy.

✔ Reposition any heavy items that the pup could pull over onto itself.

✔ Make a diligent search (perhaps with the children again) for foreign objects that a puppy could swallow. These could include thumbtacks, pins, pencils, coins, beads, and so forth. This search is especially important in carpeted areas.

✔ Check your home for any exposed woodwork, especially in older homes, that could have lead-based paint that could poison a gnawing puppy.

✔ Be certain that your puppy is not exposed to areas, furniture, or carpeting that have been treated with chemicals, pesticides, or possibly toxic sprays. This certainly includes any places where poisons may have been placed (and possibly forgotten) for rats, mice, roaches, or ants.

✔ Block off balconies, stairwells, and porches where a puppy could fall and be injured or killed.

✔ Close off any places behind televisions, upright pianos, or other heavy furniture where a youngster could get trapped. This includes railings or banisters where a puppy's head might get stuck.

✔ Puppy proofing also includes thoroughly training the entire family about what should and should not be done when the puppy is around. Care should be taken to prevent a pup from rushing out a door and into harm's way. Family members should open doors carefully to avoid crushing a little terrier behind them. No cars should move in a garage or driveway until the driver is *absolutely* certain the pup is not under the vehicle. Family members should be careful to avoid stepping on the puppy.

✔ Make appropriate use of your pup's crate (see "The Cage/Crate/Carrier," page 39).

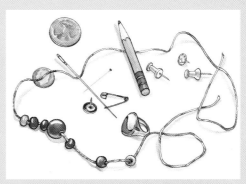

When puppy proofing, pick up any and all items that a curious pup could swallow.

✔ Most puppy proofing involves common sense. However, by taking an organized approach, you will be less likely to miss something that could injure your new family member. Protecting a new puppy should not be an afterthought, it should be an always thought. The youngster is only a few days removed from the safety of its mother and littermates. The puppy has to count on its new family to keep it from harm.

BRINGING YOUR APBT/AMSTAFF HOME

First Things First

The first few weeks and months in the life of your APBT/Amstaff will set the tone for what kind of dog it will become. The first important steps toward socializing and training your new dog must have started before you ever saw it. Initial training is done by the mother. The breeder should have started early socialization. Unless these two things have occurred, the psychological makeup of the resulting puppy may well be incomplete throughout its entire life.

The need for this early socialization underscores the importance of picking the right breeder from whom to obtain a puppy. Responsible breeders know that some human interaction must begin even before the puppy's eyes are open and must continue in a consistent manner throughout much of the youngster's first year.

Socialization

Socializing a puppy literally means introducing it to new things and people in a nonthreatening manner. This socialization process makes all the difference in whether an animal will be wild or tame and whether it will be comfortable around humans or afraid of them. All the stories about dogs being born in the wild or

Socialization during the first few months of a puppy's life is crucial, especially with the APBT and Amstaff breeds.

wild wolves becoming like lapdogs after meeting just the right human are just stories.

Animals begin to learn early as a part of basic survival. As a general rule, a dog that has not bonded with humans before it is 12 weeks old is not ever likely to do so. When the dog in question is one of the most powerful canine athletes on earth, the matter of socialization takes on even greater significance.

Amstaff or American Pit Bull Terrier puppies are like little learning sponges, soaking up information from their earliest sentient moments. Because dogs use their sense of smell even more than their sense of hearing and their hearing more than their sense of sight, the first human scents that come their way will be registered while the pups are still blind sucklings. What they hear, in terms of tones rather than actual words, will become part of their inventory of threatening or nonthreatening stimuli.

The right kind of socialization will introduce the puppies to different types of people: males, females, children, older people, and people from ethnic groups other than that of the breeder. In this way, the mental and acceptance horizons of a very young puppy are broadened to include many different humans. The puppy learns that humans, as a group, pose no threat. Some breeds become thoroughly socialized more easily than others. However, most experts agree that the canine that becomes the best companion or pet is the one that receives the best socialization.

TIP

Socializing Your Puppy

When your puppy is small, it's a very good idea to introduce him to a number of different types of animals and a variety of people. It's important not to neglect different ethnic groups, people in wheelchairs, small children and babies, and older people.

One good way to make your pup comfortable around new people is to put him in a sit (see page 79), and have a "stranger" feed your pup a treat. The puppy will soon realize that if he sits nicely and obeys, he will be rewarded with a snack. Your friends and neighbors will also appreciate the exercise because it will make them familiar with your dog, and as we know, the APBT/Amstaff can be intimidating and misunderstood before people get to know him.

If your puppy has a tremendous difficulty sitting still or receiving treats from strangers, or if he shows any signs of aggression, this could mean a problem, and you should get to a respected trainer immediately. Remember, the longer problems with aggression persist, the more difficult they become to correct.

Socialization can also take place between the puppy and other dogs, cats, and other animals that the dog may encounter in its life. Some of the herding or herd protection breeds are exposed to the smells and sounds of sheep very early in the pups' lives, which helps to forge a bond the dog will have its entire life.

The time line for socialization is crucial. Most breeders believe that most bonding with humans must begin early and, to a large extent, be accomplished within the first six weeks of a puppy's life. Authorities differ on the exact age. However, most believe that without appropriate, gentle, thorough socialization, a dog will never reach its potential as a pet or companion.

Adjustment Time

If geographically possible, you and your family should visit the puppy of your choice several times before you bring it home. By letting the puppy become familiar with your voices, appearance, and scents, it will not be leaving the security of its mother and littermates and going away with total strangers. You might also bring some breeder-approved toy for the pup to become familiar with and then take the toy with you when you go home with the youngster.

Remember that the puppy can certainly be stressed by being abruptly uprooted from the only world it has ever known. Be gentle with the new puppy. This will help it get the best-possible start in its new home. Even the trip home in a car can be stressful. This is one time that a dog may not need to be in a carrier. Have an adult member of the family securely and safely hold the puppy during the ride. (This person should wear old clothes and bring some old towels in case of motion sickness or other mishaps.)

Training your new puppy begins immediately. Some dog experts advise that you should already have an outdoor area picked out as a urine and feces relief site. You may be able to salt this location with some droppings or litter from the puppy's first home. Immediately upon arriving home, take the puppy to this site, and wait until it relieves itself. The smell of urine or droppings should encourage the puppy to do this. When it does, as it generally will, enthusiastically praise the puppy. This first natural activity will be the pup's first success and will begin its training process with you.

Your puppy should arrive at your home when it can be the center of attention and will not be neglected or ignored in any way. This pretty well eliminates Christmas puppies as a good idea unless the puppy is the only gift anyone gets that season. The puppy has no idea where it is and only vague realizations of who you and your family are. It will need a lot of love and consistent care to help lessen the trauma of this time.

Try, if at all possible, to have a responsible adult home with the puppy for the first several days to a week. Taking several days off from work to help this young, invited guest get off to a great start in your home is time well spent and can shorten this all-important adjustment time in the life of the puppy.

Your APBT or Amstaff puppy will not just automatically know the things you will want it to know any more than a human infant would be able to function without someone to guide and teach it. No one in the pup's new home should be harsh or severe toward the pup during this time. The puppy needs to learn its first lessons in its new home in a warm, trusting, and supportive environment.

The cage/crate/carrier is one of the most important purchases you will ever make—for your dog and for yourself!

The Cage/Crate/Carrier

Your American Staffordshire Terrier or your American Pit Bull Terrier will always be a better pet and companion if it remains in close contact with you. If you allow your puppy to live with you, you will discover key things about this little canine that you will probably miss or that will not even manifest themselves if the pup is relegated to a kennel or backyard existence. The pup will also learn things from being in close proximity to you that it will never learn if it becomes the dog out back.

The greatest aid to allowing your dog to live comfortably under the same roof with you and your family is the cage, crate, or carrier. Utilizing the natural instinct the dog has to be a denning creature will not only be a better way to share living quarters but is also better for the dog.

Your should purchase such a den substitute before you bring your APBT/Amstaff puppy home for the first time. After you have given the pup a chance to be a star by performing

With his toy held firmly between his feet, this stately blue-and-white male almost seems to pose for this picture.

correctly at the preset waste relief site, you can bring the youngster inside. After a few minutes of welcoming the puppy home, you can introduce what will become its own place within your household—the cage/crate/carrier.

As with the toy you might have introduced to the puppy before it left its mother and litter-mates and the urine-soaked litter or droppings to help your puppy understand the relief area, you may be able to get an old towel or blanket that has the comforting scent of its mother and siblings. Put it into the cage/crate/carrier. This will help make the new den less like solitary confinement for a new puppy.

Everyone in your family must understand that this crate is not a tiny prison. They should know that the puppy will need a place of its own and that its successful integration into the family will go much more smoothly with a crate than without. There is no cruelty or harshness in helping a puppy by letting it have its own crate. In addition, the process of housebreaking is greatly enhanced by working the natural processes relating to den behavior.

Place the crate somewhere that is out of the way but not isolated. Choose a location out of direct sunlight and out of drafts. Pick a spot that will let the puppy see what is going on in the room when it is in the crate but that does not sit right in the main walking area. Your puppy will want to be a part of things. However, the den is supposed to be a place to go to rest or to just take time out.

When you first introduce your new APBT or Amstaff to your home, let it have a chance to

Your pup's crate should be located where the dog can see what's going on in the room but will be out of the way of heavy foot traffic.

The APBT/Amstaff has quite a reputation—as an excellent pet and companion!

Socialization is among the most important things you can do for a puppy, especially a puppy that will grow up to be a powerful American Staffordshire or American Pit Bull Terrier!

get acquainted with its new family in its new surroundings. Do not roughhouse with the youngster now, play only gently. Watch the pup to see if it needs to make a trip back to the relief area. If it does show any sign of wanting to urinate or defecate, quickly and gently pick it up and head to the relief spot. If you make it in time and the pup uses the area, always praise it lavishly. This is the first step in housebreaking your puppy.

Keep playtimes brief with the puppy in the initial days. As it begins to tire, gently move it to the home-scented crate or carrier. You want the pup to associate being tired with going to this place of rest. Simply place the little one into the crate or carrier, shut the door, and walk away.

Two aspects of the APBT or the Amstaff work against each other here. These breeds generally have a lot of endurance, even as puppies. They also are generally very bright. The humans in your household have to show restraint in keeping playtimes brief and not always depend on the puppy for a sign that it is tired. Also, the puppy will learn from your consistent repetition that the crate is the place to go for a rest. Smart terrier puppies will sometimes go to the crate all by themselves for a little nap or just a short break. Associating the den with sleep is a very important lesson for your pup to learn.

Your American Staffordshire or American Pit Bull Terrier puppy will now have to adjust to life without its mother and sisters and brothers. This adjustment is one the puppy and your family must learn together.

Your puppy must learn that the crate is a place for rest and sleep. This is not important just for the breaks it will need during the day but for sleeping during the night as well! The puppy must recognize that when placed into the crate or carrier at night, it should go to sleep.

The lesson for you and your family is that the puppy must be allowed to learn its lesson. Most importantly, nobody should feel sorry for the lonely, whining, or crying puppy. If you or someone in your family responds to each whimper and cry that the lonely youngster makes, the lesson will not be lost on the puppy. Instead, your puppy will think, "If I want them to come to hold or play with me, all I have to do is cry." This is not the lesson you want your pup to learn.

A sad, lonely, crying canine baby is not a happy vision. An even sadder vision is the sad, lonely, crying canine adult that has become neurotic about being left alone at night. Being left in its crate at night will not kill or even harm your puppy. The thousands of potentially good house pets that have become neurotic and bad house pets because someone weakened at the first sound of sadness probably die in an animal shelter.

Helping Your Pup Settle In

You can help your APBT or Amstaff settle in with less trauma in many ways. You may have already started doing them by providing a toy or blanket with familiar smells on it. You can speak to a lonely, crated puppy sparingly but with a calm and reassuring tone. This will let the pup know that you are not far away.

Some breeders recommend placing some surrogate items into the crate or nearby. You might add an old hot-water bottle (that does not leak) to provide warmth. Some people have windup alarm clocks that tick loudly and simulate a mother's heartbeat. A small radio set to an all-night talk station, at a low volume, and left near the crate might give the puppy some comforting sounds. This might also be true of a tape recorder playing a relaxation tape of gentle surf and seashore sounds.

Be certain to put nothing with an electric cord into the crate or in reach of the puppy during the day. Amstaffs and APBTs, even as puppies, have powerful jaws. The hot-water bottle may not be a good idea after the first night or so.

As in so many areas of concern with these breeds, consistency in helping a puppy settle in is absolutely essential. If any member of a family shows pity for the poor, sad puppy in the crate all by itself, he or she will undo all the good that crate training can accomplish. Every family member needs to be on the same page in trying to help the puppy learn the lessons, however hard they may seem at the time.

Another key area of the settling-in process involves what the puppy eats. Unless otherwise recommended by the breeder, you should have obtained some of the same food the pup was eating at its first home. Shifting foods now can be a serious mistake and should not be undertaken without legitimate reasons. Dietary changes may bring on bowel upsets and even an increase in stress levels for the puppy. Diarrhea may come about because of the stress of the move. If it continues for more than a day or two, contact your veterinarian.

The Crucial Early Lessons

You have brought your Amstaff or APBT puppy home. It had a successful first experience (with much accompanying praise) at the relief site. Your family and you made the youngster feel welcome and happy to be in its new home. Each of you was firm in not giving in when the puppy cried the first few nights when it was in its crate. You gave it the same food that it had been eating, and its system quickly got over move-related diarrhea. The puppy, in spite of a few little mistakes, is almost completely housebroken.

You now have helped the settling in process take place. Much of what the puppy learns from now on will be additional lessons in good behavior. Consistency is vital here as in every area of pet ownership. These dogs, the American Pit Bull Terrier and the American Staffordshire Terrier, are quite intelligent and remember much more than you think they will. If a 15-pound (6.8 kg) puppy is allowed onto the couch, the same dog as a 60-pound (27.2 kg) adult will expect to be allowed onto the couch. If it is not allowed as an adult to do what it did as a puppy, it will stubbornly remember this as something inconsistent.

Dogs, like most children, are great at testing the limits. They will want to see how far they can go this time with an activity that was not clearly stopped last time. A thoughtful and caring APBT or Amstaff owner will not subject a dog to these Jekyll and Hyde actions. Simply put, a puppy must be gently, but firmly, taught the behaviors that you will expect of it as an adult. A lot of potentially great dogs in many breeds have been almost ruined by inconsistent behavior from their humans. Do not do this to your APBT or American Staffordshire!

Keeping Your APBT/Amstaff Close to You

During the first formative weeks of your relationship with your new puppy, keep the youngster close to you. The crate is an appropriate place to confine a puppy or dog when you can not supervise it, but the crate should never become a substitute for the vitally important human interaction the youngster needs. Your puppy will learn a lot by being with you. This will begin the all-important training phase of the young dog's life.

One APBT puppy (of an acknowledged pit dog strain or family) was with its new owner, a young woman, when a phone call came telling her that her father had passed away. Understandably, the young woman burst into tears. While still crying, she picked up the curious puppy and hugged and caressed it as she sobbed. She then put the youngster into its crate while she dressed to go to the hospital where her father had died. The young dog became an excellent adult pet. However, each time the phone rang or tears were shed in its home, it would go to its crate on its own initiative!

UNDERSTANDING YOUR APBT/AMSTAFF

As I said before, there is probably no breed of dog that has been as misunderstood as the American Pit Bull Terrier. Actually, this maligning has spilled over onto the Amstaff, the Staffordshire Bull Terrier, the Bull Terrier, and several other breeds as well. At best, the APBT and kindred breeds are victims of public misapprehension. At worst, these dogs meet with fear and irrational loathing.

The great rise in popularity of pit bulls, Rottweilers, and other potentially aggressive protection dogs has advanced this mentality by creating a market for such dogs. This has led to the overproduction of puppies from ill-advised breedings. This overproduction has been justified by irresponsible breeders whose goal is not improvement of a breed but exploitation of a breed for profit.

Like any dogs bred for a specific job, the need to do that job is generally still close to the surface. Cocker Spaniels from generations of show stock still pay attention to birds and may even point as their ancestors were bred to do. Collies and Shetland Sheepdogs still have definite herding instincts. Pet Beagles still have the motivation to trail rabbits and other small game. Amstaffs and APBTs were originally bred to fight other dogs. To deny that lingering vestiges of this behavior are not present within

The APBT/Amstaff is a very powerful breed of dog, but with a knowledgeable owner, it can thrive as a great family pet.

some of these dogs would be naive and untrue. To say that all, or even most, American Pit Bull Terriers and American Staffordshire Terriers are vicious, dangerous animals is also false.

Like other breeds, the American Pit Bull Terrier and the American Staffordshire Terrier will become what their breeding, socialization, training, and care (or lack thereof) allow them to become. For their size, height, and weight, there are no more powerful dogs in the world. Because of their fighting legacy, their overall musculature can be developed in either a positive or a negative way. The APBT or the Amstaff can be among the best of pets for an aware and responsible dog owner. In the hands of a malevolent, neglectful, or ignorant owner, the same dog could become a canine menace. The breeding, socialization, training, and, most of all, the owner of an APBT or an Amstaff will determine which of these dogs will emerge!

The APBT/Amstaff as Canine Companion

The American Staffordshire Terrier and the American Pit Bull Terrier can be excellent companion dogs for the caring and consistent owner. Dedication to their humans is a breed trait, but sometimes overprotectiveness is, too. The wise owner will do everything possible to foster, develop, encourage, and insure the dog's positive traits.

A well-bred, well-trained APBT or Amstaff will be an excellent family dog. Thousands of people have enjoyed them as pets without any problems. Former presidents, movie stars, and world leaders have owned APBTs or Amstaffs with nothing but good things to say about them. These dogs were family-oriented pets that represented no threat to the neighbors or to the community in general.

The problems attributed to pit bulls have generally been seen in poorly bred and poorly trained animals that had not been adequately socialized to other animals and people. A powerful, active dog (of any breed or mixture of breeds) needs to have an excellent temperament and be thoroughly trained. Without these essentials, trouble awaits.

The APBT or the Amstaff is certainly not the right pet for everyone. A powerful dog needs adequate control, and some older people and children cannot physically supply that control. A first-time dog owner should probably not buy an APBT or an Amstaff! An insecure person who wants only an aggressive dog to bolster some personal human inadequacy should never own one of these dogs. An uncaring or negligent person should not buy an Amstaff or an APBT (or any other dog for that matter).

The best candidate for ownership of an American Pit Bull Terrier or an American Staffordshire Terrier is someone who has a good understanding of dogs from personal experience. This person is usually willing to seek out just the right dog from the best breeding lines that have a family history of excellent temperaments. This potential dog owner will want to assume the socializing and training responsibilities that will help develop the dog of his or her choice into an excellent canine citizen. This prospective owner will provide good care for the APBT or Amstaff. This person will insure that the dog has the right food, lodging, veterinary care, and human interaction.

The APBT/Amstaff and Children

The well-bred, well-socialized, well-trained American Pit Bull Terrier is usually less of a threat to children than the children are to it. An overwhelming majority of dog bites in the United States involve dogs other than the APBT. Most of these bites came from toy breeds, Cocker Spaniels, and Cocker crosses. The number of bites directly relate to the immense popularity and casual breeding backgrounds of many of these dogs.

The *Little Rascals* comedy films of several decades ago featured a dog, Pete or Petey the Pup, of American Pit Bull Terrier/Amstaff breeding. This dog (or several dogs according to one source) was recognized by a circle painted around the dog's left eye. Pete was claimed by both the UKC's American Pit Bull Terrier contingent and the AKC's American Staffordshire (then simply Staffordshire Terrier) followers. Petey worked with some of the most popular child actors of the time and in the dizzying climate of a studio back lot. No serious problems caused by Petey, the American Pit Bull Terrier/American Staffordshire Terrier, have ever come to light.

Many responsible breeders of Amstaffs and APBTs raise their dogs with their children. These knowledgeable dog people train their dogs and their children to understand and appropriately interact with one another. Certainly some Amstaffs and APBTs have bitten humans, some of whom were children, but so have dogs of every breed. Some breeds are overwhelmingly greater potential biters than the APBT/Amstaff.

Teaching Your Children Dog Safety

Children need to be taught how to approach strange dogs of any breed, just as dogs need to be socialized to and with children. Children need to learn correct behavior around dogs. Children must learn not to attempt to take away a dog's food, not to approach an injured animal, and not to act in a way that could be perceived by the dog as threatening. Dogs need good training and need to be in a household where all humans, including children, have a higher ranking in the pack (see "Pack Behavior and Your APBT/Amstaff," page 71) than the dogs.

✔ Children should be taught never to approach a stray dog without a responsible adult being there.

✔ Children should be taught not to run up to a strange dog, even if the dog is on a leash.

✔ Children should be taught not to get right into the face of a dog they do not know and especially not to make direct eye contact with such a dog.

✔ Children need to learn the right ways to approach a dog so as not to threaten it, that is, quietly and from a nonfrontal direction.

✔ Children need to speak calmly to a dog and slowly offer a hand for the animal to sniff as an introduction.

✔ Children need to learn a dog's body language that says approaching may not be safe and to never approach a dog showing the following signs:

1. Aggression—ruffled hair on its back and neck (the dog tries to be as large as it can be), stiffness, ears and tail erect and not at ease, possible growling, and a generally challenging posture.

2. Frightened—cringing, ground hugging, trying to be as small as possible, tail down on the ground or held tightly between its legs, and a generally terrified or suspicious posture.

Note: Dogs exhibiting a combination of aggression and fright are often the most dangerous.

3. Injured—possibly lying down, whimpering, even loudly crying with pain.

4. A dog that is eating and that wants to protect its food.

5. A male dog intent on pursuing or even mating with a female.

6. A mother dog with puppies.

✔ Children should be taught not to run away from a dog, as this may encourage a chase.

✔ Children should avoid loud or rough playing around a protective dog.

Many, many children have grown up with American Pit Bull Terriers and American Staffordshire Terriers with nothing but the deepest love for their pets. A well-bred and well-trained APBT or Amstaff can be every bit as good a canine companion for children as any other breed. The key is to search for the well-bred dog and train it properly.

The APBT/Amstaff and Other Dogs

The ancestors of the American Pit Bull Terrier and the American Staffordshire Terrier were originally bred to fight other dogs in staged dog fights in pits. Not only did these fights require a powerful canine athlete, they also required dogs that relished such contests. Dogs that are strangers will test the limits of each other, not unlike some schoolboys on the playground. When an APBT or an Amstaff is confronted by another dog, a conflict is always possible. This is true of all breeds. That an APBT or an Amstaff

APBT/Amstaffs need a significant amount of exercise, but be sure they are always kept within a confined area.

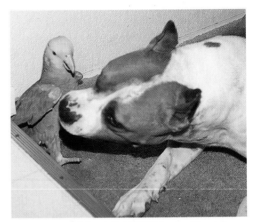

Be very careful with APBT/Amstaffs and other small animals. Properly supervised, a pair like this can be friends.

is involved should only increase the human control factors that should be always present.

Because no dog, not just an Amstaff or an APBT, should be allowed to run about freely in a neighborhood, contacts between strange dogs should always be under controlled circumstances. During walks on the street or in the park, the APBT or Amstaff should be controlled by the following:

1. A knowledgeable, aware owner who is physically and mentally capable of avoiding obvious troublesome situations.

2. Thorough training that should make the Amstaff or APBT obedient to every command, even when under considerable stress.

3. A sturdy collar and lead (leash) that an alert owner holds securely.

When describing a particular breed's interaction with strange dogs, dog book writers seem to take some pride in saying things like, "The such-and-such does not look for trouble but is able to take care of itself with other dogs." Such

remarks seem to mean that the breed under discussion will fight if given no other option and will give a good account of itself. That the APBT or the Amstaff would give a good account of itself should be taken for granted, but this should *never* be allowed to happen.

A well-known breeder of APBTs sold a promising young show and stud dog prospect to a young man and gave him strict advice to avoid physical conflicts with other animals. The man failed to heed the warning and allowed his young male to catch and kill squirrels in a city park. He then allowed it to roll (in pit dog language) or briefly fight with a Rottweiler in the same park. This male's naturally aggressive tendencies were positively reinforced. Thus encouraged by his owner, this young dog began to be more and more aggressive toward other animals. Ultimately, the dog was returned to the breeder, who spent months of intense training in an attempt to change the dog's aggressive behavior.

The APBT/Amstaff and Other Pets

A home with other pets needs to take the same wise precautions with Amstaff and APBTs that it would with any other breed. Until an adult dog of any breed understands that other pets belong in the home and are not to be chased or harmed, it must be constantly monitored by humans when in the presence of these other pets.

A puppy brought into a home that already includes other animals can be socialized to accept these other pets as part of the living arrangements. An adequately socialized APBT or Amstaff is no more a threat to other pets than would be any other dog with similar socialization and training.

The APBT/Amstaff and Guests in the Home

These dogs have ancestry that were bred to attack other animals, not other humans. In an ironic twist, the pit dog breeders enhanced this animal's aggressive behavior but would not and could not tolerate fighters aggressive toward humans. Although some poorly bred APBTs and American Staffordshires may show aggressive actions toward humans, these must be considered aberrations from the well-bred norm.

Many guests find that the only threat they face from most American Pit Bull Terriers or Amstaff Terriers is being licked to death. These are, by nature, friendly dogs that will shower a friend of the master or mistress with considerable affection. During the early preparation for this book, I was invited to a breeder's home. While seated on a couch, I observed five double-registered APBTs/Amstaffs watching me. The breeder left the room for a telephone

APBT/Amstaffs living with other pets must always be socialized, trained, and kept under the watchful eye of their owner.

Whatever this baby is doing, his canine baby-sitter is paying close attention.

call, and the dogs approached the couch. First one and then another politely sniffed my shoes and pants. Then, as if by signal, they relaxed and went about their regular activities. Two dogs, both females, stayed near me. One lay contentedly at my feet and the other, a large blue-and-white dog, put her considerable head onto my knee for petting.

Normally, a guest in the home will be accepted after being welcomed by a dog's owner. Threatening actions may attract a dog's attention. However, a friendly guest should have no cause for apprehension.

Dogs do seem to sense fear in a person. Some people have developed what amounts to a phobia about dogs in general and the pit bull specifically. If a guest has such feelings, legitimate or otherwise, perhaps a prudent dog owner should be gracious and put a dog into its kennel, crate, or some other place away from the guest.

The APBT/Amstaff and Strangers

As with guests in the home, a stranger may find APBTs or Amstaffs mainly friendly and curious. Another irony is that these breeds do not make exceptional guard dogs. Although their presence and their reputations make them a considerable deterrent to trespassers, most well-bred, well-trained, well-socialized APBT/Amstaffs will pose no danger to a mannerly stranger.

The wise dog owner keeps pets under control, thus avoiding accidental confrontations that could lead to trouble. By having a fenced yard or by keeping the APBT/Amstaff inside or in a kennel area, most negative interaction with strangers can be prevented.

The APBT/Amstaff in the Neighborhood

Stories about pit bulls abound and may impact on a pet owner's relationship with the neighborhood. That *no* APBT or Amstaff should be allowed to run loose should go without saying. Letting an APBT/Amstaff run loose shows a lack of regard for one's neighbors and is probably against the law. Using fences, kennels, and leashes makes for good neighbors.

Some communities, states, counties, and even countries have enacted legislation that bans certain breeds of dogs, among them the APBT/Amstaff. These laws are probably nonsensical in most cases because they are often unenforceable and misdirected. However, they are in place and should be taken into consideration before purchasing a dog that would fall under such legal restrictions.

Children should learn dog body language to recognize aggressive dogs and frightened dogs. Both could be dangerous.

Understanding Aggression

Many terrier breeds were bred to possess toughness or grit as it is sometimes called. The earth terriers—Scotties, Sealyhams, Jack Russells, and others—were known to go into an animal's burrow and fight or drive out the prey. These earth terriers required grit to do their job. This attitude was often associated with aggressiveness toward other animals.

Animal-aggressive behavior was a needed element in these tough, little hunting dogs. Aggressiveness toward humans was not. A terrier that would fight or attack its master was not valued, probably was done away with, and certainly was never allowed to reproduce. Animal aggressiveness had its place, aggressiveness toward humans did not.

The very mechanics of the dog pit, as distasteful as they may be, necessitated that fighting dogs be picked up and handled by their owners during the fight. A dog that would injure its handler was a liability. Pit dogs were required to be ready to fight other dogs, but they could not fight people or they were usually destroyed.

The pit dog people were among the first dog breeders to keep careful records and breed intensely for specific goals. These goals did not include viciousness toward human beings. The pit bull received its label of being vicious only quite recently. It stems from the current popularity of these breeds.

Popularity has been a curse to every breed of dog that has had to endure it. When a breed becomes popular, the greedy and uncaring people who call themselves dog breeders come along to rake in some of the cash to be made from producing pups of this or that breed. Much of this breeding is done without any regard for the quality of the breeding stock, for the outcomes of the dogs, or for the humans who buy them.

Many breeds will produce their share of dogs that are aggressive toward both animals and humans. Unscrupulous breeders have capitalized on these aggressive traits by breeding such dogs together. The resulting animals have doubly aggressive temperaments, which the breeds do not normally possess. The American Pit Bull Terrier has been the victim of this kind of breeding. Some pit bulls cannot be trusted around people or animals and should probably be destroyed.

The Amstaff and the APBT from temperamentally sound genetic backgrounds with adequate socialization, adequate training, and caring owners are not the same dogs as the vicious hyperaggressive animals produced by callous, unthinking, or greedy breeders. The best American Staffordshire and the best American Pit Bull Terrier families will produce excellent pet and companion dogs that any knowledgeable dog owner would be proud to own. Do not settle for anything less than the best!

The owner of the APBT must go to further extremes to assure the community that his or her dog is a pet, not a threat. This may be unjust, unfair, and unrealistic, but in many places, it is a fact of life. Being a responsible APBT/Amstaff owner may be more of a task than owning other dogs, but many people have found APBTs and Amstaffs well worth it!

CARING FOR YOUR APBT/AMSTAFF

Being Responsible for Your Pet

Owning a dog means more than just giving it food and water and an occasional pat on the head. Dogs in general, and APBTs/Amstaffs in particular, need to be an integral and interactive part of their families rather than relegated to the backyard.

Your American Pit Bull Terrier or American Staffordshire Terrier will need consistent and responsible care. The animal is an innocent invitee into your home and into your life. Do not make the invitation if you are not seriously willing to follow through on it! The dog cannot control the things that happen to it, but you and your family usually can.

Keeping Your APBT/Amstaff Out of Harm's Way

A dog is still a dog, even with all its good points. Dogs, like children, may not always recognize potential danger or situations where they could get into trouble. The humans in the dog's family must keep the animal out of harm's way.

Your dog will be totally dependent on you for all her needs, so her long-term mental and physical health will be a reflection on your care.

✔ Begin leash training very early with your APBT/Amstaff. These dogs are very strong pullers. One 60-pound (27.2 kg) dog, in a contest, pulled a load weighing over a ton. Children and smaller adults cannot hope to stop an energetic and enthusiastic APBT or Amstaff by body weight or brute force.

✔ Do not ever let your pet run free in the neighborhood, in the park, at the beach, or anywhere it might encounter another dog or a similar dangerous situation.

✔ By starting at the earliest age, make absolutely clear that you will not allow aggressive behavior toward another animal or human.

✔ Make sure that your backyard fence or kennel fence is strong enough and tall enough to keep an unsupervised pet in.

✔ When out on walks with your APBT/Amstaff and encountering other dogs (with their owners or without them), be smart and do not let even a minor confrontation with your dog get started. APBTs and Amstaffs are pretty smart and may remember that one time you seemed to encourage aggressive behavior. Consistency is your best training aid.

✔ Remember that just the presence of your dog may frighten some people. Do not let someone else's fear or overreaction cause your pet to become threatened. One Amstaff owner walks her pet in the early morning and will go

TIP

Picking Up a Puppy, the Right Way

As simple as it sounds, you should know several important things about picking up a puppy.

✔ Amstaff and APBT puppies are often squirmy, active youngsters. Always be sure to support the puppy's rear end with one hand while comfortably cradling its chest with the other hand. This will make the puppy feel secure and keep it from jumping out of your hands.

✔ If your children are in on the choosing process (as they certainly should be), make sure that they do not squeeze a puppy too tightly and that they follow the two-hands rule to insure safety for the pup.

✔ Do not try to hold more than one puppy at a time. If you want to compare them, have someone else hold one while you hold the other.

✔ Pay attention to the mother dog's comfort level. These are her babies, and she will want to be sure they are safe. Move slowly, and do not pick up a youngster without the breeder's permission or when the breeder is not with you.

✔ Do not pick up all the puppies in a litter. You usually do not need to handle the pups that do not fit the description of what you are seeking.

a block out of the way to avoid another pet owner with a Chow Chow that has an uncertain temperament.

✔ You and your family must protect your pet from bad situations. These include strangers who may want to see what "that bad pit bull will do." Avoiding problems will eliminate possible injuries or possible retraining of your APBT/Amstaff.

Exercise

Your pet should get regular daily exercise. This could come in the form of walks with you, romps with the children in the backyard, or in controlled runs (on leash). You do not have to run a marathon with your APBT/Amstaff because a pet in good condition that is being correctly fed will get by on moderate physical exercise.

Your dog's strong jaws will need a durable, non splintering chew toy, perhaps made of hardened rubber or nylon (see "Essential Purchases," page 31), to allow it to work off some energy chewing each day. Check with a person experienced with APBTs or Amstaffs about other forms of exercise or exercise toys that may be advisable.

Grooming

As with so many other aspects of APBT/Amstaff ownership, grooming should begin in early puppyhood both as a cosmetic activity and as a part of the youngster's training. Brushing, bathing, teeth cleaning, and nail trimming are all much easier to accomplish on a powerful adult dog that was introduced to these things when it was very young.

Grooming your Amstaff or APBT puppy should be done in a serious manner. Choose a place and a time that will be free of distractions. Handle the grooming as an adjunct to the training process. The puppy must be made to understand that this is not playtime, but it can be a pleasant time with you.

Brushing not only helps to keep the skin invigorated by removing dead hair and skin, dirt, and any foreign matter that may have gotten on the dog, but it actually eliminates the need for a lot of baths. Bathing your dog too often will actually harm the skin and coat of the Amstaff or the APBT. The skin and hair can become dried out and the natural luster and shine of the coat diminished.

Pay particular attention to the areas around the eyes and ears. These areas can be cleaned with a damp washcloth.

Regular brushing and grooming not only makes it a pleasurable experience for the puppy, but it will give you a good opportunity to discover the presence of any skin problems, minor wounds, or parasites (mites, ticks, and fleas). Your consistent attention to your pet's cleanliness needs will be amply repaid with a more presentable pet and with the additional opportunity for bonding with the animal that a few moments of brushing can bring.

Traveling with Your Pet

Going on trips with an American Staffordshire or an APBT is somewhat different than traveling with dogs of other breeds. You need to be constantly aware that your friendly pet may not be wanted or allowed in certain places. Check out the dog law ordinances of any places you plan to visit *before* you take your pet there.

The brush and comb are two of the key ingredients of proper grooming. The other two are starting grooming early and doing it often.

Whereas some locations simply do not lend themselves to taking a pet along, other sites that could be excellent for you and your dog. Your primary considerations should always be for the safety, comfort, and needs of the dog.

By Auto

Many dog-related activities, like dog shows and obedience events, involve a good deal of travel by automobile. Good canine car safety is essential if you plan to go places with your pet. You should follow some important rules whenever your pet rides with you in the family car:

✔ Keep your pet restrained in some way while traveling in a car. The best way is in an airline-type dog carrier. When the dog is secure in such a carrier, it will not be apt to be thrown about in the event of an accident, a sharp turn, or a sudden stop. Other restraints like doggy seat belt harnesses (never human seat belts around the dog or through its collar!) may provide some protection.

✔ Never let your American Pit Bull Terrier or American Staffordshire Terrier ride with its

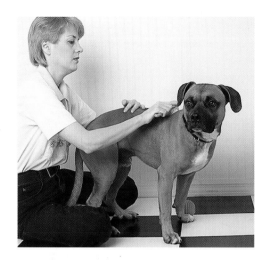

Regular grooming also gives you the opportunity to check for skin problems, parasites, and minor wounds.

✔ *Under no circumstances* should you ever leave your pet in a parked car. Even with the windows partially down, the inside of a parked car can become like an oven on a day when outside temperatures are 60°F (15.6°C) or higher. Your pet can die in a surprisingly short time under such seemingly innocuous conditions. Another reason for not leaving a pet unsupervised in your car is the chance for passersby to taunt or even release or steal it. Not everyone knows

head out a window. This may look like fun for the dog, but it is dangerous. Insects, road debris, fumes, and other negative things can cause your pet eye injuries or other problems.

Regular veterinary care is an important way to ensure that your pet stays in the best of health.

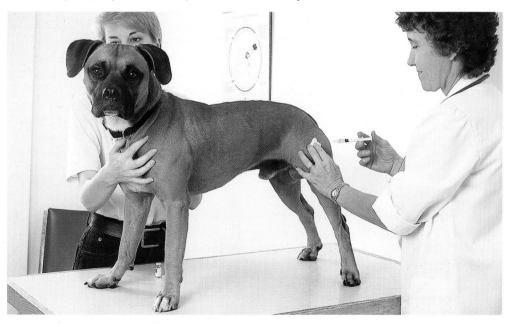

Better safe than sorry—portable pet carriers are a must when traveling with your dog.

that your pet is just out with you for a short trip. All some people will see is a supposedly dangerous dog.

✔ Do not allow your pet to ride unrestrained in the back of an open pickup truck. This may sound like an unnecessary caution, but many dogs are hurt or killed in just this manner every year. Not only does the pet stand a chance of being thrown out of the truck bed, but it may see something worthy of investigation and actually jump out.

✔ When you do travel longer distances with your pet, even with it in a carrier, check with your veterinarian first. Not taking a very young puppy, an oldster, or a dog with some health problems on the trip may be best. Your

This blue brindle looks happy to have reached his destination.

When your pet rides with you in an automobile, it will be much safer inside a carrier.

veterinarian can also advise and provide motion sickness medication if deemed necessary.

✔ Try to schedule travel breaks every hour to give the dog a little time out of the confines of the carrier, a little water, or a chance to relieve itself. Of course, always use a collar and lead when letting your pet out on these breaks.

✔ When using interstate rest areas, walk your dog only in the designated pet walks. Always be alert to possible dangers in these rest areas: speeding or inattentive drivers, stray dogs, antifreeze or other chemical leaks, broken glass, garbage, and people unfriendly to dogs.

✔ If your trip requires you to stay overnight while traveling, be certain that you arrange lodging at a hotel or motel that allows well-trained pets. Never try to slip your dog into a hotel where dogs are prohibited; you may be breaking the law!

✔ Unless you are sure that the food your APBT/Amstaff normally eats is available where you are going, carry enough food with you for the trip.

✔ Before crossing international boundaries or even some state lines, be certain your Amstaff or APBT has all the required shots (with a shot

record from your veterinarian to prove it) and possibly a health certificate. Again, because of the controversy surrounding dogs of this type, be certain you are not putting your pet into bureaucratic danger by going into certain locales where breed-specific laws may be on the books.

By Plane

Traveling with your pet by airplane is much more complex for you and potentially more dangerous for the dog than it was at one time. Of course, all the rules for auto travel apply getting to and from the airport. However, some airborne safety rules must be added:

✔ Before embarking, take your Amstaff or APBT to your veterinarian for a physical and get a health certificate (which is now required by all airlines). This certificate cannot be dated more than ten days prior to your flight date. Discuss with your veterinarian the possible use of canine tranquilizers.

✔ If the cage/crate/carrier you normally use with your APBT/Amstaff is not an approved air-line model, you should arrange to rent one from the airline. Check over the carrier (yours or theirs) to make certain that it is in good shape and that the door and latch work. Other than the conversion kit, which allows a pet to be watered from outside the carrier, do not put any food or water into the carrier.

✔ Prudently arrange your flight as directly as possible to avoid having your dog shifted from plane to plane. Even if you have to drive some distance to a hub airport for a direct flight, it will be preferable. (Some airlines charge quite a

bit more if they have to off-load your pet from one flight and then load it onto another.)

✔ Always fly on the same flight with your pet. If your Amstaff or APBT gets bumped off the flight, get off yourself and arrange for another plane where you can go with your dog. When you make reservations, carefully discuss your travel plans, including your dog, with the airline personnel. Be sure you understand all that is required of you. Be firm! Be sure they understand all that you expect of the airline and its employees. Get names and write them down.

✔ Be early for your flight time; airlines usually require that pet passengers be checked in no later than two hours before the estimated time of departure.

✔ Insist on seeing your APBT/Amstaff actually loaded onto the airplane. You can be courteous, but remain quite firm with the airline workers. This is your pet, and it matters a great deal to you. To them it may be just another dog they have to transport. Let them know you seriously intend for the dog to be safe and comfortable.

Leaving Your Dog Behind When You Travel

If you have assessed the situation and find that your pet will be better off not going on a trip, you have several options for leaving your pet behind.

Boarding

Boarding your American Pit Bull Terrier or American Staffordshire Terrier is often a good alternative to the stress of travel. Many excellent dog-boarding facilities are in the United States. Many of these are affiliated with the American Boarding Kennel Association (ABKA) (see "Information," page 108). The ABKA maintains strict standards to accredit boarding kennels.

Pet Sitters

You may be able to find a professional pet sitter right in your hometown who will enable your dog to stay in its own home. Always use only bonded pet sitters, and always check references.

Friends or Relatives

You may be able to avail yourself of friends or family members to feed, water, and check on your dog while you are away. Be sure that the person you choose is fond of the dog and vice versa! One alternative is your dog's breeder, who might be willing to let an old friend return for a visit.

Also note: Your veterinarian should already be a friend of your APBT/Amstaff. The dog will know the animal doctor and the staff of the clinic. Many veterinarians will board pets for their clients, or at least recommend a qualified facility for you to leave the dog.

FEEDING YOUR APBT/AMSTAFF

Balance—The Basis of Proper Nutrition

Your pet must depend on you for many things. Of these things, nothing is more important than a balanced diet. If your APBT/Amstaff's food is deficient in any area, your dog may not be able to reach its full genetic potential. A balanced diet will be scientifically formulated to contain all the key elements a canine needs to survive and thrive: proteins, carbohydrates, fats, vitamins, and minerals. All of these must be in the proper proportions for a particular dog at a particular stage of its life.

The Importance of Quality and Consistency in Feeding

Finding a good-quality dog food that meets the nutritional needs of your APBT/Amstaff may require some effort on your part. Seek information and valid opinions from several sources. Discuss foods and feeding with your veterinarian. You might also talk to a knowledgeable pet products retailer. Do not leave out experienced APBT/Amstaff breeders in your quest for the right food.

This blue brindle pup has a way to go to catch up to his large friend, and proper nutrition is the only way he'll get there.

Finding a quality dog food that your pet will enjoy is only part of the search for good nutrition. How you feed your pet is as important as what you feed it. Consistency is a crucial part of a good diet. Continually switching dog food brands will undo all the good of striving for a balanced diet. All dog foods are not the same. All quality foods differ in some aspects. When you find the food that seems to be right for your dog, stick with it unless some problem develops that can be directly traced to the food. Your dog is a creature of habit. When you change foods unnecessarily, you not only unbalance the dog's diet, but you can stress your pet for no good reason.

By feeding a quality, nutritionally balanced product in a consistent manner, you will actually help your dog avoid many food-related problems like diarrhea and developing a picky appetite. Your pet does not really want, nor does its system need, wide variety in its diet.

Also, it is very important to stick with a regular feeding schedule. Your dog should have its own food dish and a specific location, either inside or outside, for that dish. Your dog should receive a regular amount of the quality food it likes. Do not double up some days and skimp at other times. Dogs are animals of routine. Feed them on a routine basis to get the most out of the dog food and the dog.

The Building Blocks of a Good Diet

A balanced canine diet is comprised of several component parts that together ensure nutritional completeness. If any of these parts is absent, overdone, or out of kilter, then the entire diet is not doing what you want and what your dog needs. The following describes these parts in detail.

Proteins

The first ingredient in the guaranteed analysis (that must be included on all pet food labels) is the percentage of proteins. Proteins bring to the diet the amino acids that are so important in helping to develop and then maintain your dog's sound bones and healthy musculature. Proteins also aid in the healing and repair of injured bone and muscle.

Proteins help your dog's body produce antibodies, which fight against infections. Necessary enzymes and hormones that aid the chemical functioning of the dog's body also are provided for by proper levels of proteins in a pet's food.

Carbohydrates

Along with fats, the carbohydrates in a dog food formula provide the needed sources of energy to keep the dog functioning at its best. Carbohydrates are usually added to a dog food through some thoroughly cooked grains, vegetable items, or processed starches. Although not as concentrated a source of energy as are fats, carbohydrates are still one of the key building blocks to a successful diet.

Fats

Not only do the fats in your pet's diet provide double the usable energy of the same amount of carbohydrates, fats are also a delivery system for important vitamins. The fat-soluble vitamins, A, D, E, and K, are essential to overall good health. Fats are useful in helping maintain a dog's nervous system. Fats also help to promote a healthy skin and a shiny coat.

Another important role that fats play in pet foods does not directly relate to health maintenance but to palatability. Simply stated, fats make dog foods taste better to dogs. If the food is tasty, the dog is apt to eat it more readily. No matter how good a food may be nutritionally, if a pet will not eat it, all the built-in nutritional quality is wasted.

Vitamins and Minerals

Modern premium dog food manufacturers have done an exceptional job in providing the appropriate levels of vitamins and minerals in pet foods. Both vitamins and minerals, like calcium and phosphorus, are important for the development and maintenance of a dog's body and bodily functions. As important as both vitamins and minerals are, they can be easily overdone by a well-intended but ill-informed dog owner. Unless recommended by your veterinarian, leave vitamin and mineral supplementation to the experts. A balanced diet has already enough of both for the health of your pet.

Water

One of the most important building blocks in a good canine nutrition program is pure, fresh water. An active terrier like the Amstaff/APBT will need lots of clean water available to it at all times. Your pet will not consume enough water if it is hot from the sun, algae laden, or dirty to keep your Amstaff/APBT in the best of shape. A dog owner has no more important job than keeping water bowls clean, away from the heat of the sun or the cold of the winter, and filled with fresh water.

Feeding APBT/Amstaff Puppies (Under Two Years Old)

APBT puppies need a diet that will enable them to grow up strong and healthy. A number of quality puppy foods can give puppies that extra start on life.

Puppy feeding tip: Whatever puppy food your pup was eating when you got it is the puppy food you should probably continue feeding. Unless a problem develops that can be traced directly to this food, *do not change it!*

Consistency is even more important with puppies than with adult dogs. Puppies will need to be fed about four times each day at regular times and in regular amounts. As they grow older, puppies can gradually get by on three and then on two feedings per day. Always discuss feeding changes or problems with your veterinarian or with a trusted and knowledgeable APBT/Amstaff friend.

Feeding the Adult APBT/Amstaff (Two to Eight Years Old)

Different families of American Pit Bull Terriers may mature faster than others. It is always important to know as much about the family or strain of APBT to which your dog belongs as you can. An adult dog will not normally need the same level of proteins and fats that a

growing puppy will need. Continuing to feed a puppy diet could cause an adult dog to gain too much weight. Adult diets need to be formulated for the normal nutritional and maturational needs of adult dogs. If your terrier is used for showing, hunting, breeding, or for any rigorous activity, it may need more nutrition than the average adult diet can supply.

Finding the right food for an adult dog will depend on quizzing your APBT friends, your veterinarian, or others knowledgeable about both terriers and about general pet nutrition. Adult dogs can do well on about two feedings per day, but some dogs will need more food per feeding and some less. Any adult canine-feeding program must be tailored to fit the needs of the individual dog and not simply be based on some broad recommendations for all dogs or even for all American Pit Bull Terriers or American Staffordshire Terriers. As with puppies, your dog will do better when fed a consistent diet of the same food.

Feeding the Older APBT/Amstaff (Over Eight Years Old)

Although some dogs are still in their prime at age eight, this is usually a good time to start observing subtle metabolic changes in a dog. A dog that ate three cups of a particular food per day at age four may have been considerably more active at that time than at age eight. The level of exercise has much to do with the ability of a dog to burn up the energy that its dog food provides. Because fat is one key energy source, it is reasonable to assume that if a dog does not use most of the fat in its diet, the fat will stay with the dog. Obesity is one of the greatest killers of dogs. A fat dog cannot truly be considered a healthy dog.

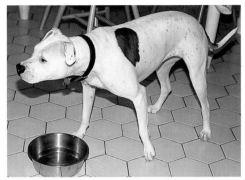

These APBT/Amstaffs need a balanced diet with premium quality pet food, lots of fresh water, and NO table scraps!

carbohydrates as the prime energy source. Although some gradual shifting may be necessary, largely due to the loss of the main agent making the food palatable—fat, a change from adult food to senior food can be accomplished in time.

Feeding Spayed Females and Neutered Males

Spaying and neutering is an excellent idea for any American Pit Bull Terrier or Amstaff not actually used for breeding. The need to feed these altered animals in a different way is important. As a rule, spays and neuters become more like older dogs in their general metabolism. This possibly stems from the lower metabolic rate than in nonspayed or nonneutered dogs' lives.

Do not assume that a spayed or neutered animal will automatically become obese. As terriers, APBTs and American Staffordshires will be more active than many breeds. A dog owner

A number of lite or senior dog foods are on the market. Discuss these with your breeder friends and with your veterinarian. The level of average activity of your dog is always a good gauge for the necessity of shifting to an older dog diet. In general, these foods for older dogs tend to move away from fats and more toward

that has had a pet fixed should monitor the condition of the animal closely and make the necessary dietetic adjustments if the dog begins to put on weight. Usually, good continued exercise and the avoidance of both table scraps and overfeeding is enough to keep most spays and neuters in good shape.

Fighting Obesity

As mentioned, fat dogs are not really healthy dogs. This is probably even truer for a dog of action and activity. Not providing table scraps can certainly help keep a dog's diet balanced. Making a feeding plan fit the dog rather than the other way around can also help keep obesity away. Plenty of good exercise and never overfeeding will usually do the rest for an American Staffordshire/APBT.

When You Change Dog Foods

There are several opinions as to the best way to change dog foods. One clear area of agreement centers on doing the change as gradually as possible. Rapid shifting will bring on diarrhea and other problems. Any dietary changes should be for valid reasons and not because you liked an advertisement or won a bag of some new food in a raffle. If and when you change, try to blend the new food in with the existing diet.

One way to change a dog's food gradually is to take one month to do it and add in increas-

ing percentages of the new ration in graduated amounts. For example, during the first week of the month, you feed 75 percent of the old food with 25 percent of the new. During the second and third weeks, you feed a 50/50 mixture of new and old. During the final week of the month, you feed 75 percent of the new food and 25 percent of what had been the

It's important to realize special dietary considerations for puppies (above) and older dogs (below). Older dogs, especially, shouldn't be carrying around any extra weight.

dog's food. Carefully observe each week for loose stools, food rejection, or other problems. If none exist, by the end of one month, you should be able to feed 100 percent of the new food on a continuous basis.

Other percentage-mixing methods exist, but this one offers both a very gradual approach with an easy-to-follow time frame. As with all matters concerning your terrier's diet, take changing it seriously!

Different Types of Dog Food

Far too many pet owners consider dog food as an afterthought or minor point in owning a dog. Nothing is further from the truth. One of the things you should know about any food is how digestible it is. Generally the better-quality brands will result in less waste in the yard or kennel area. Additionally, dogs will actually eat less of a quality food.

Canned

Canned or wet dog food is the most palatable form of dog food. It is also the most expensive, the most prone to produce smelly and messy stools, and the most likely to contribute to obesity if overfed. Canned foods are usually quite meaty in their appearance and have a lot of great aromas that dogs seem to relish. If a pet is started exclusively on canned food, shifting to other types of food later is often quite difficult. Canned food also is between 75 to 85 percent moisture and can spoil quickly at room temperature. Dogs fed canned food exclusively often have more dental problems than dogs fed a dry, crunchy food.

On the plus side, canned dog foods have the longest shelf life. They are convenient and require only a can opener to be of use. They can be purchased in one-meal increments or by the case and have fewer storage problems than one might see in some climates with dry foods.

Canned foods can be fed as a complete diet or, as is more often the case, as a mixer or additive with dry foods. Most owners of APBTs who feed canned foods probably do so as only part of a diet and in combination with some other type of dog food.

Semimoist

Semimoist foods come in foil or plastic-wrapped packaging and in a great many meaty-looking shapes. They have the convenience and nearly the palatability of canned food without the high moisture levels. Semimoist diets usually have moisture levels around 30 percent. Semimoist dog foods are also somewhat expensive. The stool quality produced by eating such foods is not usually as good as with a premium-quality dry food. Some brands of semimoist foods also contain sugar and artificial colorings.

Semimoist dog foods do serve well as mixers with dry food. They are also good travel foods or as occasional treats. Semimoist foods are also good for dogs whose zest for eating is a little off. However, an exclusively semimoist diet is, like a totally canned food diet, easy to overdo. Fat dogs often result from such feeding.

Dry

Dry dog food is the overwhelming favorite of most breeders of larger dogs. Not only is dry food usually more cost-effective, but it also gives the best digestibility of all the types.

Good digestibility not only results in a cleaner kennel or backyard area, but a dog will not have to be fed as much. Feeding less food can help stave off the great enemy—obesity. Dry foods keep well without refrigeration (which is not true for canned and semimoist foods). Palatability for dry foods is not as good as with the other types. However, premium foods are generally well accepted by dogs that have been given some dry foods from puppyhood on. Introducing dry foods into the diet of a dog that has eaten only canned or semimoist products or table scraps all its life is much more difficult.

Although no food or treat item should replace regular dental care, dry foods do help reduce film and tartar buildup and do exercise a dog's gums. Dry foods have an advantage over canned or semimoist foods in that they can be perfectly adequate as a complete food source throughout a dog's life. Pups that have been introduced to a good-quality dry food will generally eat it well and do well on it. Because dry foods have a moisture rating of only about 10 percent, you must provide the dog with plenty of clean, fresh water.

Treats

Dozens of dog treats are on the market. Most of these will be readily eaten by a dog. However, only some of them are formulated so that they will not throw off the all-important balance of a dog's diet. When searching for a treat for your APBT, remember that a treat for a dog can be like dessert for a child—it can be overdone. Try to find a treat that will give an APBT a chance to exercise those strong jaws as well as provide something a little different.

Table scraps are not treats and should not be given as such. Human goodies like cookies and candy also have no place as a treat for a dog. Some of these, like chocolate, can actually do a dog real harm as well as unbalance the pet's diet.

Read the labels on treat items as carefully as you would on a dog food. Try to find a dog biscuit or similar product that seems to match the items found in your APBT's regular food most closely. Use treats on a limited basis only, and never overdo it!

Home Cooking

You might think that the most caring way of feeding your dog is by making its meals with your very own hands, but that is not the case. Unless you are a skilled canine nutritionist with years of experience in successfully feeding dogs, home cooking can be just another name for table scraps.

The dog food industry has spent millions upon millions of dollars to perfect their products. The average dog food on the market today will be, in all probability, a much better ration for your American Pit Bull Terrier or your American Staffordshire Terrier than your best efforts in the kitchen. Why not turn your efforts to researching which commercial food will be best for your dog and let the experts' experience work for you? Your dog will nearly always do better on a balanced diet formulated by professionals. Unless you are a professional, leave dog food making to them.

TRAINING YOUR APBT/AMSTAFF

Train Your Dog or It Will Train You!

Any dog of any size will need appropriate training. Failure to provide this training will usually result in a poor companion animal. A poor companion animal is a danger to itself or to other creatures—human and animal. Training for the APBT and Amstaff is an important enough consideration to make it an absolute. *Do not own an untrained American Staffordshire Terrier or American Pit Bull Terrier!*

I once knew two pet owners who went to great expense to purchase a top-quality puppy of one of the giant breeds. These owners gloried in the beauty of this big youngster, but they were unwilling or unable to commit themselves to train it. The puppy grew into a magnificent 200-pound (90.7 kg) adult that ruled the household. Although he did not come from a strain or family that had evidenced bad temperaments, this big guy clearly became dangerous to be around. He would do only what he wanted to do and would enforce his will with a growl or snarl.

This dog's owners were terrified of him. They could not control him. However, they were deeply mortified and mystified when a dog-

Every pet should be trained, but this is especially true with the APBT/Amstaff. A properly trained pup will develop into a better, safer dog.

training expert actually recommended having the dog euthanized because corrective training seemed impossible. The owners were convinced that the dog was simply bad or that they were cheated on their purchase. Neither of these assumptions is true. The owners did not train the dog. Therefore, because nature hates a vacuum, the dog trained them!

This sad outcome could have been avoided with good training early on. Allowing what could have been an excellent pet to become a headstrong, untrustworthy danger is ludicrous. Training is as important as any other aspect of pet ownership. To neglect training, especially of a powerful animal like an Amstaff or an APBT, is foolish.

Special Considerations for APBT/Amstaff Training

The popular misconception of the pit bull breeds is that they are not trainable. Some consider them killer guard dogs and nothing else. Nothing could be further from the truth. The Amstaff/APBT are usually extremely bright, very trainable dogs that really want to please their owners.

Like socialization, training for an American Pit Bull Terrier or an American Staffordshire Terrier must come early. Experts suggest training begin at several months of age for some breeds—but not the APBT/Amstaff. Knowledgeable APBT/Amstaff people assert that for their pets, training must begin at a few weeks of age, not months.

Because of the dog's strength and personality, many of the things you will want a 60-pound (27.2 kg) adult to know and do must be taught when the APBT/Amstaff is a 15-pound (6.8 kg) puppy. Training cannot begin too early. One top Amstaff breeder has her puppies already showring trained by as early as eight weeks of age! These youngsters will obediently walk on leash, stand still to be evaluated, and allow their teeth and gums to be checked.

Training these dogs does not have to be quite as repetitive as for some other breeds. When the pup apparently understands a command, do not overdo the repetitions. A puppy that becomes bored or jaded with a command will stop paying attention, and learning actually stops.

One of the best ways to continue socialization into training is to take the still young puppy out into the world to expose it to sounds, smells, noises, and other stimuli that it will certainly encounter later. One breeder believes in taking a youngster (after it has been immunized) to dog shows, obedience trials, shopping centers, and

other very public places. By putting a puppy into these often confusing surroundings while it is still young, the puppy will not be frightened in similar circumstances later.

By safely controlling the pup's introduction to sometimes frightening stimuli, the owner can reassure the young animal and let it know that no harm is coming its way. A puppy given the right exposure and reinforcement while still a young puppy will be easier to train and easier to handle as an adult.

One significant and sometimes controversial method of working with Amstaff or American Pit Bull Terriers involves the area of animal aggression. Many experts in these breeds stress that an aggressive action on the part of a puppy toward another dog simply cannot be tolerated! A fairly common approach to handling this cardinal sin for the pit bull breeds is to snatch up the puppy immediately, really making a strong impression on its young mind. The puppy is abruptly lifted off the ground by the owner and is held eye-to-eye with its master or mistress. A strong tongue-lashing follows. The puppy is made to understand in no uncertain terms that aggressive behavior cannot and will not be allowed. As one Amstaff breeder stated, "You have to make the punishment so unpleasantly memorable to the puppy that it will *never* forget what brought that punishment on!"

You have no reason ever to strike the puppy. The rude pickup, the eye-to-eye challenge, the angry demeanor, and the harsh words should

Never allow a young APBT or Amstaff to show aggressive behavior to another dog or a person. Pick up a puppy and get its attention immediately to let it know such aggressiveness will not be tolerated!

be enough. Many breeders report that one such encounter is all a puppy needs to set in its mental processes that aggression toward other dogs will get it into real trouble with the boss!

This tough and immediate response may seem harsh, but it is in keeping with training methods used by the first and best trainer any dog could have—its mother! Mother dogs are rarely subtle when reproving their pups. They do not harm the little ones. However, they make it abundantly clear that certain actions will bring immediate, consistent, and appropriate consequences! This mother-to-pup training is an extension of the natural pack behavior deeply ingrained in all canines.

Pack Behavior and Your APBT/Amstaff

Your American Staffordshire or APBT will be a loved member of your family. Your family is not your pet's first family affiliation. Your American Pit Bull Terrier or Amstaff is also a pack member just like wolves and other canines. The pack is the most important part of a dog's life. It is the natural caste system or pecking order that dictates where each and every dog fits in.

Wild dogs will form hierarchies identical to that of wolves. The pack has a clearly defined rank-ordering system with each animal at its own level, dominant over those below it on the ladder, subservient to those above it. The leader, identified as the alpha or first male, is usually the biggest, strongest, most keenly intelligent dog in the pack. All other pack members bend to the will of this leader unless they are ready to challenge him for the top spot.

Pack behavior is something that your APBT/Amstaff will usually already understand when it gets to your home. It learned this concept from its mother. In fact, a pack superstructure with its mother, siblings, and the breeder was already in place. The mother dog is always the leader of her litter pack, but the siblings work out who is next in line and so forth.

Understanding pack behavior is crucial to training your pet. Like using denning behavior in crate training, pack behavior can be used to make certain that your American Pit Bull Terrier or Amstaff knows its place within your family and is content with the arrangement.

In the dominant giant breed example discussed previously, serious problems occurred when the pack leadership in a human family was taken over by a dog. Your pet, of whatever breed, must be at the bottom of the ladder, with all the humans above it. The giant breed dog in the example was clearly the pack leader in its home and dominated the two human members who lived there. Even if this dog was of a tiny toy breed, this turnabout of the human and canine relationship would be a very serious problem.

Within your home setting and throughout the life of your APBT/Amstaff, you have to be the dominant leader. You have to fill the alpha slot. The other members of your family or household will be the other pack members, with the dog fitting in neatly as the last one on the list.

The pack is not some power game everyone plays against the dog. Pack membership for a canine is as natural as any other instinctive behavior. It serves as an important ballast in the dog's life, providing the security, appropriate rank placement, and sense of belonging that dogs need. A well-adjusted, well-socialized American Pit Bull Terrier or

You must be firm when training your APBT/Amstaff, but it's also important to train without anger.

American Staffordshire Terrier needs to understand where it fits within its social universe. You, or some other responsible human, will have to assume responsibility for seeing that this natural chain of command is instilled in your family and remains in place.

You can observe pack behavior in any grouping of dogs. Two dogs meet for the first time. They stand rather stiff legged, often going through the sniffing ritual. Unless a fight is imminent, one dog will recognize that it should be subservient to the other. The subservient dog will assume submissive demeanor and do submissive things to show it is no threat to the dominant animal. Some of these submissive behaviors are cringing, offering no defense, rolling over on its back, or even releasing small amounts of urine.

Build on the Mother Dog's Training Model

Training your American Staffordshire or American Pit Bull Terrier will be considerably quicker and easier if you build on the training the pup's mother has already done. The model for training that she used is an excellent one for you to adapt. Following her example will make you a better trainer and your APBT/Amstaff a better pet.

Fairness: Each puppy in the litter got equal treatment. No puppy was able to get away with a transgression for which another would be punished. The punishment meted out by the mother was also fair and appropriate for the misdeed.

Immediacy: A wayward puppy was punished immediately while the youngster's short attention span could still associate the misdeed with the subsequent reprimand.

Without anger: The puppies were punished without anger. The mother dog's actions were not designed to injure the pups but to mold their behavior. She also did not subject a miscreant pup to long periods of incessant barking to correct its behavior.

Consistency: The puppies were able to learn from the consistent manner in which their mother acted. A transgression did not receive punishment on one occasion and a reward the next time. The youngsters came to understand that certain misdeeds would bring about certain punishments, each and every time.

With love: The puppies were reproved and corrected in a secure and nurturing environment. An earlier misdeed did not force a puppy into exile. The love of the mother and the support of the littermates were not withheld as additional punishment.

A well-adjusted Amstaff or APBT mother will have built a firm foundation for the future training of her offspring. By following her model of fairness, immediate response, absence of anger, and consistency in a loving environment, you will find your pup much easier to train.

How Dog Training Works

The mother's example provides humans with insight into how dog training is actually accomplished. Dogs learn by having negative actions corrected and having positive actions rewarded and reinforced. If a puppy jumps up onto a couch and gets a firm "No" and is gently, but very definitely, removed from that

The five major components to training your APBT/Amstaff—fairness, immediacy, lack of anger, consistency, and correction with love.

couch, it will soon get the idea that the couch is off-limits. If one member of the family lets the puppy get onto the couch, the pup will only become confused and possibly resentful when it is reprimanded and removed.

The keys to training are as simple as the mother dog's model: fairness, immediacy, a lack of anger, consistency, and correction with love. Many schools of thought about dog training exist, ranging from harsh methods using shock collars to quasi training that really only lets the dog do what it wants to do. However, the mother's model is one constant that many approaches have at their center.

Housebreaking

Your APBT or Amstaff will be a much better pet if it shares your home. For this reason, one of the most important and earliest lessons you will want your puppy to learn is when and

where it is appropriate to relieve itself. When the great biological need to urinate or defecate is combined with a puppy's desire to please you, the puppy is undergoing some powerful and often conflicting stresses. You can work with these stresses to assist the pup in becoming housebroken or go against these strong pulls and run the risk of the youngster never becoming the in-house pet it could have become.

Regardless of how much you may want the puppy to become housebroken or how much the puppy will want to please you, puppies physiologically have limited bladder control until they are four to six months old.

A special issue for APBTs or Amstaffs centers on the fact that some female puppies seem to be a little easier to housebreak than their little brothers. Perhaps this is because of the relatively high pain threshold of the Amstaff or APBT, along with the terrier-like focused curiosity of the young males. Many breeders observe that male puppies get so absorbed in playing, exploring, or whatever they are doing that they do not always exhibit the discomfort signs of needing to relieve themselves in time to prevent an accident. In any case, the females are quick studies in the business of becoming housebroken, with their male siblings only a week or two behind them in learning speed.

The housebreaking learning process began when you took the new puppy to the special relief spot and then enthusiastically praised it when it urinated or defecated there. Note that because not all puppies gain bladder control at the same time and because a difference possibly exists between males and females, expecting perfection is unwise. If you are consistent and gentle with an APBT or Amstaff puppy of either gender, it will soon learn this important lesson.

The cage/crate/carrier that was crucial in helping your puppy settle in takes on equal importance in the housebreaking process. Because of the innate desire for a puppy not to soil its sleeping place, the crate is the last place the youngster wants to mess up. Crate training (see page 75) will make the task of housebreaking much easier on you and the puppy.

Paper Training

A less effective and certainly less efficient way to housebreak a puppy involves the use of newspapers placed all over the floor in some easy-to-clean room like a spare bathroom or a laundry room. Rather than someone being available to help the youngster make it outside to the relief spot, the puppy is placed into this papered room and left there.

Crate training makes housebreaking so much more easy to accomplish that paper training is almost an unnecessary discussion. However, it may be called for with some people. Some lifestyles make taking a puppy from its crate and hustling it outside to the relief site difficult. Apartment dwellers, for example, may find taking a pup down several flights to a preset location rapidly enough difficult.

Other people find they must leave the puppy alone for several hours or even all day. You could not leave a very young puppy in its crate under such conditions. Paper training is a substitute but not really an equal substitute to crate training/housebreaking. It will be slower and less attuned to the way the adult dog will need to function. However, if used consistently, paper training does provide an alternative of sorts.

Paper training involves confining the puppy in the papered room. It does not work particularly well with the crate-training/timed outside visit method because the puppy will suddenly be given two right places to defecate and urinate rather than the one special site. Paper training will require:

✔ Three distinct areas in the confinement room:
1. a waste elimination area;
2. a food and water area;
3. a sleeping or rest area where the puppy's crate is located.

✔ The floor of the waste area should be covered with several layers of spread-out newspapers. Using layers will allow the top sheets to be soiled or wet and then removed. The pup's scent will remain behind on the lower layers and will thus encourage this as the relief place.

✔ Because puppies naturally will not want to urinate or defecate near their food, water, and sleeping areas, these should be as far away from the waste area as possible.

✔ Because paper training is less effective, whenever possible praise the pup for using the waste area (as you would if the pup were at the relief spot outside).

✔ Paper training and outside visits early in the morning and late at night can be combined. Always be lavish with praise if the puppy defecates or urinates outside.

✔ A further way to combine the less effective paper method with the more effective use of an outside area is to make the waste area in the confinement room smaller and smaller as the pup matures. Gradually, a pup or young dog can be transferred completely outside. This will require a complete deodorizing of the room and a shift to the crate-training/outside trip method.

Crate Training

Crate training works because your Amstaff or APBT puppy almost instinctively will not want to mess up its den or sleeping area. The puppy will normally learn this behavior from its mother, who would chastise an older puppy who made a mess in the litter's sleeping quarters. In the wild, canines do not want to let the smell of feces and urine be a draw for predators, so denning areas are not normally fouled with urine and feces. Crate training takes advantage of two very strong innate behaviors: denning behavior and the desire to keep a den area clean. By encouraging these behaviors, you can make crate training not only convenient and useful for you but natural and comfortable for your pet. Remember the following points about crate training:

✔ Keep a positive attitude about crates. Knowledgeable dog owners know that the crate is a place of refuge for a puppy or a dog, not a cruel prison.

✔ When you purchase a cage/crate/carrier for your Amstaff or American Pit Bull Terrier, bear in mind that the small puppy of today will be the sturdy, medium-sized dog of the near future. Buy a crate for the adult dog. Use temporary partitions, usually available where you buy the crate or easily made, to keep the crate the right size for a growing puppy. If the crate is too large, the puppy may develop a waste elimination area in the corner away from where it sleeps. Keep the crate just big enough for the growing youngster.

✔ Place the crate into an out-of-the-way, but not an isolated, place in your home. This location must be away from highly changeable temperature fluctuations, drafts, and direct sunshine.

✔ Put the puppy into its den when it needs to rest and for a few hours when you will not be around to supervise it. Always take the puppy out of the crate and outside as soon as you return home.

Paper training may not be as good a method as the "relief spot" method, but it works well for pet owners who can't immediately get outside when the dog needs to evacuate.

puppy that training is serious and not just part of playtime.

✔ Taking the puppy out of the crate should not become a reward. Do not praise the youngster (except at the relief spot outside) for 10 or 15 minutes after you let it out of the crate.

✔ Make the crate comfortable for the pup by placing a sleeping mat into the crate. These mats are made to fit every size of cage, crate, or carrier and come in many washable colors and designs.

✔ Do not put food or water into the crate. This will only promote a messy sleeping area. Food and water are best kept elsewhere.

✔ If the youngster whines, barks, or cries in the crate, use a calm, authoritative voice to quiet the puppy (see "Helping Your APBT/Amstaff Pup Settle In," page 42).

✔ Be certain that all members of your household understand what the crate does and what crate training is all about.

✔ While training your pup, return it to the crate for a half-hour break before letting it out for a play session. This will imprint on the

Basic Training

Your American Pit Bull Terrier or American Staffordshire Terrier will need early and consistent training. By remembering that some puppies mature faster than others, you will be able to find a good time to begin a serious approach to teaching your pup the basic things it must learn in order to live with a family.

Because some strains or families within the American Staffordshire Terriers and American Pit Bull Terriers have different levels of maturation and trainability, you will want to involve your breeder-mentor in helping you decide when to begin with your puppy. Because these breeds often need very early work to get them off to a good start, you will need this friend's opinion about how your particular pup is progressing.

Potential training concerns may surface in different Amstaff or APBT lines. Some strains are known to be more animal aggressive than others. Listen to the advice of the breed experts that you have come to know about how best to initiate training with your puppy.

You will want your APBT or Amstaff to learn five basic commands. These commands will give you a good level of control over your young puppy, which is a crucial element of successful ownership of a dog of one of these breeds. These commands are: sit, stay, heel, down, and come. Each of these commands involves a different level of training. Each will be useful in everyday pet ownership.

The Essentials of Training Your Puppy

Establish a regular training schedule each day: Training sessions do not have to be long. Between 10 and 15 minutes for each session is sufficient.

Keep the sessions geared toward training: Avoid places and times with distractions that could draw away the full attention of your puppy. Although these times should be enjoyable, they are not times for play.

Fill the alpha role: The firm, businesslike sound of your voice will let the puppy know training time is different from playtime and that you are in charge. Be stern and consistent, but remember never to attempt training when you are angry or upset over something.

Set clear and attainable training goals: Before each training session, set definite, but reasonable, things you want to accomplish in this session. Do not expect too much too soon. Make training a matter of small, incremental steps that will ultimately move you and your Amstaff/APBT puppy toward a specific direction. (Training hint: Go over with your family what each training session is going to try to teach your puppy. Make sure they understand that they can confuse and set back the progress of a youngster by doing things that undo the training.)

Conduct each session as a single-focus class: You know that your APBT or American

When training your pet, be sure to maintain a regular daily schedule.

Staffordshire terrier may not respond well to a lot of meaningless repetitive commands. You also know that each session must have a beginning point and an ending point. Try to end each session in a positive way.

Stick to your planned goals for that session: When you train your puppy, you can go back over previous lessons. However, if the goal for today is heeling, focus on heeling. Correct your pup each time it does not heel correctly. Praise it each time it does heal right. If your APBT or Amstaff pup begins to chafe with the repetitions, cut the session short.

Reward the right way: Although some animal trainers use small bits of food as a reward during training, other dog trainers recognize that praise is what the dog wants most. When a youngster correctly does what it was commanded to do, give it an enthusiastic pat and

warm word of praise. Doing the right thing once does not mean that you and your puppy can begin playtime.

Separate training time from fun time: You want to keep your pup's attention on what it must learn. Put a little distance in the pup's mind between the training session and any subsequent play. Praise a trainee for doing the right thing. However, wait until later to show lavish affection as you play with your beloved pet.

Follow the mother dog's example of correcting immediately: Like the mother dog, you should make corrections right then, right on the spot. Waiting to correct a puppy later is useless because the youngster may not even remember the misdeed.

Consistency—the key to good training: You may be only an amateur training your first dog. However, if you are consistent, doing the training the same way each time, you will get better results than an experienced professional who is inconsistent. The young dog will need to know that the stern alpha voice you use during training means that this is serious. If you use a different tone or different words in the basic commands, the puppy may never know what you are implying.

Patience is the greatest virtue in training: As important as consistency is, without patience you are lost. Regardless of how good an American Pit Bull Terrier or Amstaff puppy you think you have, it is still just a puppy. It may want to learn from you to gain your praise. However, if you push it faster than it can go, you could ruin a fine young animal. Always be patient, both with your pup and with yourself as a trainer.

Avoid immediate training sessions after long periods of crate confinement: Puppies will usually have a lot of pent-up energy at this time and will find concentrating on their lessons difficult.

The Right Training Equipment

Training equipment for your Amstaff/APBT will consist of the following items:

A training collar: Although commonly misnamed a *choke* collar, the training collar is both humane and effective when used correctly and appropriately. This collar is for use only during training sessions. When correcting pressure is applied with a slight snap, the dog's head will come up and its attention will be brought back to the training. Combined with a stern "No," this training collar not only controls and corrects, it lets the pup know that it did something wrong. This collar should be large enough to go over the widest part of your puppy's head with no more than an inch leeway. This collar is, as previously stated, not for regular wear. The puppy should associate the training collar with the serious business of learning. This chain collar could also become snagged on something and cause the youngster to be injured if the puppy wears it all the time.

A training leash (or lead): Along with the training collar, you will need to purchase a 1-inch-wide (25-cm-wide) lead (commonly called a leash) that will not be used on your regular walks with your Amstaff or APBT pup. This, like the training collar, is just for training. It should be made of leather, nylon, or woven web material. It should be 6 feet (1.8 m) long, be of very sturdy construction, and have a comfortable and strong hand loop on one end. On the other end should be a brass or stainless steel swivel snap that can be attached to the ring on the training collar.

Let your puppy become thoroughly familiar with both the collar and the lead before you actually begin using them. These two items are important tools of the dog trainer's trade and should be of good quality. The Amstaff or APBT puppy should not fear or dislike these tools. They should signify that training time is here.

The Five Key Commands

Before You Begin Training

Just like a drill sergeant about to train some new soldiers, you need to have a command voice to best get your orders across. Before you begin training, you will need to develop such a voice to differentiate between you as a trainer and you as the pup's pal. Practice the following verbal skills:

Firmness: Give one-word commands in a clear voice to your dog, always using the dog's name before each command to get its attention, "Gunnar, sit." Be firm and businesslike. Do not use baby talk or pet nicknames. Playtime is later. This is training time.

Consistency: As in so many other areas of APBT/Amstaff ownership, consistency here is very important. Use the same tone of voice each and every time so that your tone as well as your voice will reinforce the seriousness of this training time.

Be specific—do not issue a string of several commands at one time: "Gunnar, come

In one continuous, gentle motion, pull the puppy's head up as you push its hindquarters down, giving the firm verbal command "Sit" as you do so.

here and sit down." This will only confuse the dog. Each command should be a single, specific word pronounced the same way and in the same tone each time.

Use the mother model: Remember that the puppy's first training came from a real expert, its mother. Follow her example:

1. Correct misbehavior immediately.

2. Be consistent.

3. Never lose your temper.

4. Reward with enthusiastic praise.

5. Always be patient.

"Sit"

Because your puppy will already know how to sit, your main role is to teach it when to sit and where to sit. The sit is a good first lesson for your puppy to learn because so many other basic and even some of the advanced obedience commands begin or end in this natural position.

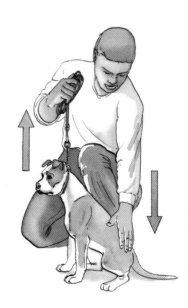

The training collar should be around the pup's neck and correctly attached to the leash or lead. Start the sit with the youngster on your left, next to your left leg. Take up all but about 12 inches (30 cm) of the excess lead. Hold the lead in your right hand. In a smooth, continuous, gentle, but firm upward move, lift the puppy's head so that it is facing a little above horizontal. As you do so, gently press downward on the pup's hindquarters. The lift of its head combined with the pushing down on its hindquarters will force the young dog to sit down as you give the command, "Gunnar, sit."

Be careful not to push down on the pup's rear end hard enough to injure or frighten the youngster. You only want to make it sit, not hurt it. After the puppy does sit, give it lots of praise. Just like with doing its business at the relief spot, you want the puppy to associate the praise with the action. This is the basis of dog training.

Remember to stick with one command at a time when training—confusing the dog is very counterproductive.

Try the sit several times, remembering the three important parts:

1. slight upward pressure on the lead and collar to lift up the pup's head;

2. gentle downward pressure on the pup's hindquarters;

3. the sit command given at exactly the same time you do the other two.

Do not overdo the first few sessions. Do not keep a puppy sitting too long or tire it or bore it by a great many repetitions. Keep the sessions interesting and enjoyable for the puppy.

Your bright American Staffordshire or American Pit Bull Terrier puppy will probably catch on to the sit very quickly. When the pup does, it will want to gain your approval and your praise and will soon be sitting on its own, even without the lead and training collar!

"Stay"

After your APBT/Amstaff has mastered the sit, it is ready for the next command, the stay. This command actually begins with your pup in the sit and really cannot be learned until the first lesson is firmly a part of what your young dog knows.

The stay begins with the puppy sitting next to your left leg. The lead is again in your right hand and is used to hold the head of the youngster up. While using your firm, alpha voice, give the command, "Gunnar, stay," as you step straight forward away from the sitting puppy, leading with your right foot. At the same time, bring the palm of your left hand down in

The "stay" command.

front of the young dog's face in a reverse of the well-known police hand signal for stop.

The stay will require four coordinated parts done at precisely the same time:

1. your gentle lifting pressure on the lead to keep the pup's head up;

2. your step forward, beginning with your right foot;

3. your left hand being placed, palm downward, in front of the dog's face;

4. your clear, firm vocal command, "Stay."

The stay is a conflicting command for a youngster. It loves you and wants to be with you, but it wants to please you by doing what you want. The stay forces the pup to choose pleasing you over staying with you.

Some American Staffordshire Terrier or American Pit Bull Terrier puppies will easily learn the stay, but others will have some trouble with it. If your pup does not stay at first, do not overdo this command the first few stay training sessions. You can try it several times. If the puppy has trouble, go back to a few sits. Let the puppy end each session with some successes and the praise reward these successes should always bring.

Patience is needed in teaching a very young dog this conflicting command. Take your time. Remember, this is just a young puppy you are working with. Be consistent in how you give the command, pull up on the lead, step away, and put your palm in front of the pup's face. Your efforts will pay off, and your puppy will stay.

The length of the stay a puppy executes may not be very long at first. Gradually, the puppy will learn to stay where you want it to and you can move farther and farther away. Remember to praise the puppy for any length of stay.

Once the pup can handle this fairly tough command, you can insert a cheerfully given release word, "OK," which will let the puppy know that it can do what it really wants and come to you and be rewarded.

"Heel"

Being able to walk with your pet at the correct place by your left leg will be a useful thing for a young puppy to know. The heel takes on added importance with the APBT and the Amstaff because these dogs are often real pullers. Teaching a very young APBT or American Staffordshire not to attempt to drag you along behind it is a crucially important skill. You will be able to control the pulling and tugging of a little pup, but a 60-pound (27.2-kg) dog can probably tow all children and most adults. The time to teach the heel is while you still have the upper hand and are stronger than your terrier.

Like the stay, the heel begins in the sit position. Both the sit and the stay must be mastered by your pup before you should attempt to teach heeling.

Hold the lead, still attached to the training collar, in your right hand. The puppy should be sitting alongside your left foot. As you give the clear, alpha-voiced command, "Gunnar, heel," step off, leading with your left foot this time. If the puppy does not move forward when you do, pop the leftover loop of the lead loudly against the side of your left leg and keep on walking. The lack of your palm in its face, plus your movement with the left foot rather than the right, combined with the gentle forward pull of the lead on its collar should cause the pup to move along with you.

When the puppy starts walking with you, praise it, but keep on moving. Keep praising the youngster as long as it stays with you, right by your left side. If the puppy has problems with this command, do not drag it all over the yard attempting to get it moving. Start the heel lesson again by going back to the sitting and staying positions and following the steps of the command:

1. hold the lead in your right hand, with the pup at a sit, and step out with your left foot;

2. use a firm voice and give the heel command;

3. gently apply forward pressure on the lead; if the pup does not move, snap the lead sharply against your leg to get its attention and keep moving;

4. praise the move and continue the praise only as long as the pup moves with you.

When you stop, give the sit command. The puppy will want to walk along with you. Since the heel makes this possible, it should be fairly easy for your Amstaff/APBT to learn. Teach the heel the right way each time, correcting the puppy immediately if it tries to lag behind you, branch off in another direction, or run on ahead of you. You have to be the one who chooses where you walk and how fast you will go. As with other lessons, make this enjoyable, but be consistent and patient.

"Down"

The down command has its beginnings with the sit and the stay. It has some aspects of the stay in that you want the pup to remain in this one spot. It differs from the stay in that you use downward pressure on the lead this time, instead of upward pressure. You want the pup's head and torso to go down to the ground or floor and for the animal to lie on its stomach.

While using your right hand, pull down on the lead while making a strong, repeated

Preparing for the "heel" command.

The "down" command.

downward motion (not unlike slowly bouncing a basketball) in front of the dog's face. At the same time you do these two things, you give the clear, firm command using the dog's name as in "Gunnar, down."

When the puppy has reached the belly-on-the-ground position, heap on the praise. The down is made easier because it is a natural position that the pup already knows. Your role is to teach the pup to do the down when you command it to do so. The constant but gentle downward pull of the lead in your hand will force the young dog to comply with your wishes.

The down is another command that must be taught to the APBT/Amstaff while you still have the leverage and greater power to teach it. You could have quite a time trying to teach the down to an adult American Staffordshire or American Pit Bull Terrier that did not want to do it. Start young to make this command as automatic as possible.

Your goal in this command is to be able to get your puppy and later your adult dog to go down onto its stomach upon hearing you give the verbal command and to stay there until you have given the "OK" release word. This command can be taught only by a consistent and patient trainer.

When the puppy starts obeying this command, do not intentionally or accidentally abuse the down by leaving a youngster in the position longer than a few minutes. Gradually you can lengthen the down periods. Keep the early sessions short and fun for the dog. Later the down should be like the stay, with the dog remaining in position (no swiveling around or rolling over onto its back) until the release word is given. If

the puppy does not stay down or moves around, correct it. When it does do a good down, for however long, provide a reward of praise.

"Come"

All dogs know how to come to their master or mistress, do they not? This may be true when the dog itself wants to come to you. However, the come is very important in that it stresses that the young APBT/Amstaff is to come to you each and every time you give the command.

Along with patience and consistency, the come will require enthusiasm from you. You should always call the dog by name, "Gunnar, come!" When beginning to teach this command, let cheerfulness blend with your firmness of voice. Make this command to a very young puppy an invitation to come to the person it loves. Spread your arms out wide, and call the puppy to you using the appropriate

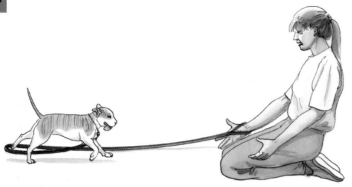

The "come" command.

the command to come with
a happy outcome when it
obeys, not with the possibility that it will be punished or
scolded for something. As
you should never scold or
reprimand a puppy or dog
at the special waste relief
site, you should never use the come to get the
animal within reach so you can do something
it will not like. If you need to punish or reprimand, go to the dog, do not try to make it
come to you.

command. When the youngster does what it
really wants to do, that is come to be with you,
give it a lot of praise.

The come can be misused and a puppy or
dog actually taught to ignore the command.
Never call your APBT/Amstaff to you to punish
it or reprimand it! Never allow anyone in your
household to do this. The puppy must associate

One way to teach the come to a young
and possibly inattentive puppy is by using the
regular lead or even a longer training lead of
20 feet (6.1 m) or more attached to the training collar. Exert gentle pressure while bringing
the pup toward you combined with the happy,
enthusiastic come command. Lavish praise
reward when the pup obeys.

Never underestimate the vital importance of
the come command and your American Pit Bull
Terrier or Amstaff's immediate obedience to it.
This one command, if instantly obeyed, can
keep a young or headstrong dog from trouble
or even death. An Amstaff or an APBT that will
not come immediately on command should
never be allowed off a leash or out of a fenced
backyard or kennel.

Do not use the come command too much as
the puppy could become bored or jaded at
numerous repetitions of it. One good way to
use it is to surprise the puppy when it is doing

*Be sure to exhibit praise when your pup
obeys a command.*

Not unlike many bikers, APBT/Amstaffs have to prove they are not the unsavory characters they are often branded.

something else, playing or running in the backyard. Give the come command when the youngster is not expecting it, and then heap on the praise for quick obedience.

Obedience Classes

Although your training efforts will normally be sufficient, you should avail yourself of any dog-training classes conducted in your area. Not only will you and your pup learn more quickly, you will do so with experienced trainers who have dealt with any problems that may arise for you and your pet. These training classes are usually held at night in some easily accessible place and have much to offer you

and your American Staffordshire or American Pit Bull Terrier.

Your puppy will gain socialization skills by being around other humans who like and understand young dogs. It will be given exposure to other dogs that are there for the same training. This will give you a chance to observe, under tightly controlled conditions, the level of animal-aggressive tendencies that your young APBT/Amstaff may have. This is an extremely valuable piece of information for you to have! One lifelong breeder of dual-registered American Pit Bull Terriers and American Staffordshire Terriers made this observation pertaining to obedience classes, "I highly recommend them to even the most experienced dog owners who are getting an Amstaff (or APBT) for the first time and I absolutely will not sell a puppy to a first-time dog owner unless they agree to faithfully attend classes."

HOW-TO: HOUSEBREAKING

Crate training will play the role it does in housebreaking when you know when your puppy will most need to void waste or urine. You should plan trips to the relief area based on this knowledge. After the puppy drinks some water or eats some puppy food, the additional pressure on its bladder or colon will mean a trip outside is needed. Follow these suggestions to help your puppy:

✔ Take the youngster to the appointed waste place after each meal or drink.

✔ Plan a trip there after periods of prolonged active play.

✔ Take the pup out of its crate and go to the relief spot as late at night as possible.

✔ Take the puppy out as early in the morning as you can.

✔ Although very late or early trips may become less necessary as the puppy grows up, plan on relief breaks several times a day whenever the dog is in your home.

✔ Recognize the telltale signs that a puppy or dog may give when an outside trip is needed:

1. A general look of discomfort or anxiety on the dog's face.

2. Circling in one spot as if looking for a clue where to go.

3. A dog that stays near the door going outside.

4. Whining and whimpering and running toward the door to get your attention.

5. The dog or puppy going into a squatting posture.

✔ If the puppy cannot wait, you should gently, calmly, but quickly pick it up and go to the relief spot even if it has an accident. At the relief spot, wait until the pup defecates or urinates there and then praise it enthusiastically.

✔ Thoroughly clean any soiled spots. Make use of scent removers since canines are motivated to use a spot where the smell of previous urine or feces remains.

✔ *Never* speak harshly or punish the puppy at the relief spot for any reason. This is a place where the puppy needs lots of little victories and rewards of praise from you. Do not confuse the youngster with correction at this special site.

✔ *Never* rub a puppy's nose in its messes. This does nothing positive for the puppy's learning and only gets it dirty.

✔ *Never* strike a puppy with your hand, a rolled-up newspaper, or anything else! This especially applies to a natural activity like defecating or urinating. This will only make the pup fear you and will actually slow down learning.

✔ Screaming at a puppy in the act of making a mess in the house is futile. You might gain some time to get the youngster outside by clapping your hands and saying a firm "No," which may break its concentration on making a

Great aids to housebreaking your pup are automatic outside visits after eating or drinking, late at night, and first thing each morning.

Another sign of needing to go outside is squatting behavior, especially near the door. Again, hurry the puppy to the right place for it to void.

mess. Rush the pup outside, and praise it when it goes where it should.

✔ Feed a high-quality puppy food that provides excellent digestibility. The stools produced by this kind of food will generally be smaller and firmer—an added benefit if an accident does happen—and easier for the dog to hold, thereby decreasing accidents.

✔ Avoid snacks and table scraps. These items will not only unbalance the pup's diet but will hinder your effort to time when trips outside should occur.

✔ Do not leave food in the Amstaff or APBT pup's food bowl all day long. This will also throw off your relief trip schedule. Pups generally do better on several small meals each day.

✔ Do not put food or edible toys like dog biscuits into the crate. Let the crate be a place of rest and/or confinement and have somewhere else for food.

✔ Do not leave your APBT or Amstaff puppy overly long in its crate as this will be painful for the youngster that may try to keep from voiding waste in order to keep the den area clean.

✔ Be consistent with your housebreaking efforts, and see that others in your household are also. Consistent training will teach most American Staffordshires or APBTs what housebreaking is all about.

✔ If you have a fenced backyard, never just turn a puppy out alone to relieve itself. Your praise is the reward for going at the right place and the right time.

✔ Playtime should not begin outside until the pup has used the relief area. Going outside must signify waste relief and not play to the youngster.

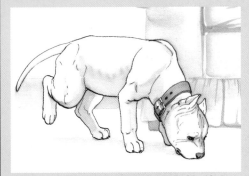

A puppy sniffing and circling is probably about to void. Watch for this behavior, and hurry the youngster outside.

MEDICAL CARE

Developing a Wellness Plan for Your Dog

Good health for your American Pit Bull Terrier or American Staffordshire Terrier will not just happen. You need to be proactive to keep your dog healthy and to shield it from injury. Your pet will give you devotion, affection, and fun-filled hours. However, it will have to depend solely on you to keep it healthy and safe.

Your Amstaff/APBT will deserve a carefully considered plan to keep it in good shape and let it live out its natural life span. Do not leave the health of this trusting, canine member of your family to chance. Concentrate on discovering those things that can harm your pet and then eliminate or deal with them. You may not be able to do this without the help of some other knowledgeable people.

A Health-Care Team

The APBT or Amstaff puppy that you have invited into your home will greatly benefit from a group of concerned humans who have its best health interests at heart. This team could consist of the following members:
✔ You, and the members of your family, will be the first line of defense for your puppy in so

Keeping your APBT/Amstaff happy and healthy should be the number one priority of pet care.

many areas. You will choose a pet from a strain or family that is as free as possible from genetically transmitted diseases and uncertain temperament. You will puppy proof your home to prevent accidents from happening to a curious and ignorant puppy. You will provide adequate housing, fencing, training, and other controls to keep your pet from hurting itself or others. You will obtain top-quality veterinary care, food, and knowledgeable advice to help your pup grow into a healthy, well-adjusted adult. You will share your lives with this dog, love it, and let it love you.
✔ An experienced Amstaff/APBT breeder will serve as a friend/mentor and help you learn to become a responsible, aware dog owner. This knowledgeable person will perform the valuable function of seeing your pet often enough to recognize traits and other specific things about it but rarely enough to be objective about certain aspects of the dog's health, training, or care. This APBT/Amstaff mentor will help you know the best paths to take in helping your pet reach its potential—in the showring, in obedience trials, as potential breeding stock, or as a first-class family pet.
✔ Your veterinarian will be the fulcrum on which the health of your American Staffordshire Terrier or American Pit Bull Terrier may balance. Find a veterinarian who knows and likes these dogs and has some experience with them. (This should not be hard, as veterinarians are often some of the staunchest supporters of the

APBT/Amstaff.) Depend on this professional's expertise in immunization, health problem prevention, and treatment. Follow the suggestions, prescription instructions, and treatment plans worked out by your veterinarian.

Preventing Accidents

Much of the preventive focus depends on common sense, anticipating problems, and heading off problems. Puppy proofing is one form of accident prevention. Keeping your APBT/Amstaff under the control of sturdy fencing, strong leashes and collars, and good training is another facet of stopping accidents before they happen. Spaying and neutering pet-quality Amstaffs and American Pit Bull Terriers can be accident prevention, in several senses of the term.

Keeping your terrier out of potentially dangerous spots (like a parked car on a warm day or running off leash in a city park) is definitely accident prevention. Recognizing that animal aggression is part of the genetic makeup of

some Amstaffs or APBTs and dealing with this before problems occur is also in this category. Recognizing that dogs of these two breeds tend to drown more often than do many other breeds can lead an owner to prevent this senseless type of fatality. Protecting your Amstaff/APBT puppy or adult from becoming poisoned from common household chemicals is good accident prevention.

Preventing Illnesses

Your American Pit Bull Terrier or American Staffordshire Terrier is from an extremely short-coated breed and may suffer from cold weather more acutely than some other breeds. Protect your pet from cold temperatures by letting it live indoors with you. If it must stay in an outside kennel, provide a thoroughly insulated and draft-proof doghouse.

You and your veterinarian can help eliminate much in the way of parasites and, in so doing, eliminate some of the health problems that can stem from flea, tick, and worm infestations. You can do your part at home to keep your pet away from unhygienic conditions and away from stray animals that may harbor communicable illnesses.

Immunizations

Getting your Amstaff or APBT immunized against the wide spectrum of illnesses that attack canines is a key part of your wellness plan for your pet. In some cases, these shots are not options but are mandated by law.

Your American Staffordshire Terrier or APBT may have had its first immunizations when it was about six weeks old. These shots may have been administered while the puppy was still

Be certain that you and your veterinarian keep your puppy up-to-date with its immunizations. This could save the youngster's life!

under the breeder's care. You should have a clearly annotated record of just what shots your new pet had at that time. The first round of immunizations were vaccinations for distemper and measles and possibly for parvovirus, canine hepatitis, leptospirosis, parainfluenza, coronavirus, and also bordetella.

Even if your youngster was immunized for all these illnesses, it will still need follow-up shots at eight to ten weeks and again at 12 weeks. Normally, the puppy immunizations end with another group of shots at 16 to 18 weeks.

Note: A number of experienced American Staffordshire and American Pit Bull Terrier breeders assert that pups of these breeds may need even additional immunization protection due to what they believe is a breed characteristic that makes young Amstaffs and APBTs harder to immunize. This is an area of concern that can best be discussed with your veterinarian and your knowledgeable breeder-mentor.

When you take your new puppy to the veterinarian for the first time, take along its medical record that the breeder should have supplied. Your dog's doctor will need to know what immunizations and other treatments this puppy may have received. Take care of these early documents as they form the nucleus of what should be your pet's lifelong health records.

When your veterinarian sets up an immunization schedule for your young APBT or American Staffordshire, follow it with the greatest of care. The best puppy from the best breeder out of the best strain of American Pit Bull Terriers or Amstaffs can die in an amazingly short time if you have not been diligent in getting immunizations done at the recommended times.

Common Ailments in the APBT/Amstaff

Distemper

One of the oldest enemies of the canine, wild and domestic, is distemper. At one time, this widespread and extremely infectious viral killer was the greatest known threat to puppies and young dogs. Entire kennels were wiped out by distemper.

Today, an immunization program has greatly decreased the incidence of distemper. Distemper, although more controlled now than decades ago, is still deadly when it has not been immunized against. Distemper is still very much in evidence among wild canines and in places where vaccination for it is inadequate or nonexistent.

A dog not completely immunized against distemper may show clinical signs as early as a week after being near an animal with the disease. At first, distemper looks like a cold with a runny nose accompanied by a slight fever. Dogs will often stop eating and exhibit fatigue, listlessness, and diarrhea.

Rabies

Rabies is one of those diseases that brings about nightmares of loving pets being transformed into ravening, foaming-at-the-mouth, canine demons bent on biting anything and everything around them. Rabies is made all the more frightening because it can be transmitted to humans and to most other warm-blooded mammals by the saliva of an infected animal, which is usually passed by a bite. In 1885, the French scientist Louis Pasteur developed a vaccine for this great dread. Until Pasteur, rabies

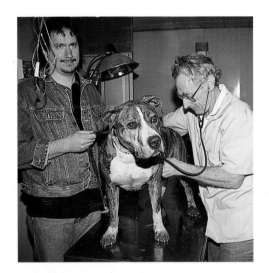

Regular visits to the veterinarian for shots and treatments will keep your pet healthy and robust.

animals die while still in the furious mode, but others live to go into the second phase. This is often called the dumb phase, which ultimately ends in paralysis, unconsciousness, and finally death.

Failure to keep a dog immunized against such an infectious and horrible killer is negligent and unlawful. Protect your puppy, your family, and yourself by making certain that your puppy gets immunized at three to six months of age. Also be sure that your pet gets its second shot at about one year of age, with annual to triennial shots for the rest of the dog's life!

Leptospirosis

Leptospirosis is a bacterial disease that primarily damages the infected dog's kidneys. In advanced cases, it can severely injure both the liver and the kidneys, causing jaundice, sores in the dog's mouth, a loss in weight, and a general weakening of the dog's hindquarters.

Leptospirosis is commonly spread by drinking water contaminated by an animal with the disease. Clinical signs of this illness are loss of appetite, fever, diarrhea, abdominal pain, and vomiting. Immunization followed by an annual booster shot will protect your pet from leptospirosis.

Hepatitis

Infectious canine hepatitis is not the same illness that humans can contract. The canine version can affect any member of the Canis family and can range in severity from a deadly

meant certain death in the most hideous manner imaginable!

One of the classic indicators of rabies was supposed to be the other name by which this dreaded killer is known—hydrophobia or fear of water. Paralysis of the laryngeal muscles that control swallowing will bring on excessive salivation or foaming at the mouth. The dog does not fear water as much as it is unable to drink and swallow.

Rabies in companion animals occurs fairly uncommonly now due to an aggressive immunization plan. It still occurs in populations of wild animals, skunks, raccoons, foxes, and stray or feral dogs and cats. England has largely been able to eliminate any incidence of rabies because of its natural oceanic boundaries and because of a vigorous quarantine that kept out many potential carriers.

Rabies has two stages or phases. The first, often called the furious phase, is so named because the inflicted animal may attack anything with which it comes into contact. Some

viral infection that can kill a dog within one day's time after it is diagnosed to a fairly mild disease.

This infectious disease can be spread by coming into contact with the urine or feces of a dog inflicted with infectious canine hepatitis. Clinical signs of the illness are listlessness, abdominal pain, tonsillitis, increased light sensitivity, fever, and bloody stools and/or vomitus.

Infectious canine hepatitis can be prevented by a good immunization program followed by annual boosters.

Protect your dog—and your family—by ensuring that your pet receives a full cycle of immunizations between three and six months of age.

Parvovirus

Young puppies especially fall victim to parvovirus, but this viral disease can take the life of an unimmunized dog at any age! Parvovirus primarily attacks the immune system, gastrointestinal tract, and heart along with the bone marrow. Young animals with this disease can suffer severe dehydration due to profuse bloody and watery diarrhea and vomiting. From onset of the disease, parvovirus can kill an affected dog or puppy within 48 hours.

Immediate medical care can save some parvovirus-stricken dogs and puppies from death. However, an effective immunization program can spare most from ever contracting the disease. Annual boosters should follow a puppy vaccination for parvovirus.

Parainfluenza

This highly contagious virus can spread rapidly through a litter of puppies or through a home with several dogs. Parainfluenza is thought to be spread by contact with infected animals as well as through the air. This disease causes tracheobronchitis, which causes a dry, hacking cough followed by repeated attempts to cough up mucus.

Parainfluenza alone is not usually very serious. If tracheobronchitis is left untreated, it can sufficiently weaken a victim and leave it vulnerable to other infections. The best course of action with parainfluenza is immunization in the puppy series of shots followed by annual reinforcement by booster. A dog or puppy with parainfluenza is usually treated by a veterinarian in isolated conditions to prevent the spread of this disease.

Coronavirus

Both puppies and adult dogs of all ages can become victims of coronavirus. This contagious disease, which is characterized by severe diarrhea with loose, foul-smelling watery stools tinged with blood, can rapidly debilitate a dog or puppy. In a condition weakened by coronavirus, an afflicted animal can contract parvovirus or other infections. An Amstaff or American Pit Bull Terrier with coronavirus can be successfully treated, but prevention through immunization is again the best course.

Bordetella

The bacterial infection bordetella often comes along with a bout of tracheobronchitis. When a bordetella infection is present, it can complicate the treatment for tracheobronchitis. An immunization can usually prevent or lessen the severity of both bordetella and the parainfluenza infections that cause tracheobronchitis.

Borelliosis (Lyme Disease)

Borelliosis, or Lyme disease, affects many mammals including humans. It is a serious, potentially fatal illness believed to be spread primarily by the tiny deer tick to dogs or to dog owners.

Although originally identified in and named for Lyme, Connecticut, this disease, which carries the medical name of borelliosis, has now spread to many parts of the United States. At one time, only hunters and hunting dogs were considered prime candidates to be infected. However, you or your dog could contract this ailment in a city park or even in a suburban backyard.

Clinical signs of Lyme disease include swelling and tenderness around joints and a loss of appetite. If you or your APBT/Amstaff have been bitten by any tick, you would be wise to seek a professional medical and veterinary opinion as soon as possible!

Other Possible Health Problems

Anal Sac Impaction

On either side of a dog's anus lie the anal glands. Normal defecation usually empties these glands, but sometimes they become clogged or impacted. When impaction occurs, these glands must be emptied of their strong-smelling secretions by hand.

One sure sign of anal gland impaction is the scooting motion seen in an affected dog as it drags its rear end along the floor. Your veterinarian can handle this concern, or you can easily learn to do it yourself.

Diarrhea

Some diarrhea is common in dogs and puppies. It may be caused by stress, food changes, or internal parasites. Diarrhea can also signal the onset of some serious illness. Any diarrhea that continues for more than 12 to 24 hours should alert you of the need for a trip with your pet to the veterinarian.

Vomiting

Like diarrhea, some vomiting is to be expected. Excitement in pups after eating may bring it on. A change in diet or added stress may cause vomiting.

Also like diarrhea, vomiting can signal that something more serious may be happening within your dog or puppy. Vomiting and diarrhea can lead to dehydration, which can put a young pup's life into peril rather quickly. Any vomiting that continues over an extended period (more than 12 hours) should trigger an automatic visit to the veterinary clinic.

Bloat (Gastric Torsion)

Bloat, or gastric torsion, is a very serious health concern for all deep-chested breeds of dogs, which includes the American Staffordshire Terrier and the American Pit Bull Terrier. Bloat can painfully kill an otherwise healthy dog in just a few hours. It involves a swelling and torsion (or twisting) of the dog's stomach from water or gas or both.

Bloat is still somewhat of a mysterious ailment. A lot of causes are suggested that may work independently of each other or that may combine to cause bloating. Some of these include the following:

✔ A large meal, particularly of dry dog food, followed by a large intake of water, followed by strenuous exercise.

✔ A genetic predisposition in some breeds and even within some strains or families within a breed.

✔ Stress from any of several sources.

✔ The age of the dog. Dogs over 24 months old seem to be more likely to bloat than do younger animals.

✔ The gender of a dog. Males seem to be more affected by bloat than do females.

From whatever cause, bloat is a real killer of deep-chested dogs. Although the American Pit Bull Terrier and the Amstaff are apparently not quite as susceptible as Bloodhounds, Great Danes, and some others, enough APBTs and Amstaffs die from bloat to make it something you will want to know about. Some clinical signs of bloat include the following:

✔ Obvious abdominal pain and noticeable abdominal swelling.

✔ Excessive salivation and rapid breathing.

✔ Pale and cool-to-the-touch skin in the mouth.

✔ A dazed and shocky look.

✔ Multiple attempts to vomit, especially when nothing comes up.

A dog with bloat needs immediate care if it is to have a chance of surviving. First, alert your veterinarian. Then safely transport your dog to the clinic.

Canine Hip Dysplasia

One of the most discussed and cussed canine health issues for modern dog owners is CHD, or canine hip dysplasia. CHD does not have the life-threatening immediacy of many of the common canine diseases or of gastric torsion (bloat). However, it can be quite debilitating and painful for a dog that has a severe form of this condition.

By description, CHD is a medical condition in which the hip joint is slack or loose. This slackness or looseness is combined with a deformity of the socket of the hip and the femoral head joining the thighbone. This malformation in the development of the hip's bone and connective tissues leaves an unstable hip joint. Instead of a strong fit like a cup for the end of the thighbone, the CHD-affected hip is often quite shallow. This condition can cause an unsteady, wobbling gait that can be very painful.

Much has been written about the possibility of CHD being an inherited disorder. This may be only partially accurate, for not every puppy born of a dysplastic sire and/or dam will have the condition. Conversely, even normal or non-CHD parents can produce some dysplastic offspring.

CHD cannot be determined with any degree of certainty until a dog is around two years old. The Orthopedic Foundation for Animals (OFA) has developed a widely used X-ray process used to determine if CHD is present in a dog and the degree to which it is present. Some veterinarians may also be able to pre-screen for CHD by using the Penn hip testing method on younger dogs.

American Staffordshire Terriers are fairly high on the list of breeds that have a relatively high incidence of hip dysplasia. Some disagreement exists among American Pit Bull Terrier and American Staffordshire Terrier breeders about just how valid the CHD testing is for their dogs. One breeder asserted that many APBTs and Amstaffs judged to have CHD by the OFA testing never seem to develop CHD. A prominent Amstaff breeder (of double-registered dogs) produced an OFA test for a particular American Staffordshire that was significantly worse than an OFA test on the same dog submitted for testing as an American Pit Bull Terrier!

Regardless of whether some breeders are more prone to believe their dogs are not afflicted with CHD quite to the degree that testing may seem to indicate, CHD should be a matter of concern.

Canine hip dysplasia is not necessarily life threatening, but severe cases can be very painful for your dog.

The better the CHD test scores on your pup's parents, the better your chances seem to be of getting a youngster that will not be crippled by this painful condition. CHD is just another reason for taking your time when you set out to find the right American Pit Bull Terrier or American Staffordshire Terrier puppy.

Allergies, Skin Problems, and Coat Problems

Some dogs in every breed seem to become the victim of every allergy and skin or coat problem that comes along. The presence of inherited conditions is something you will want to avoid in your puppy. One reason for seeing the parents of your puppy is to assess their appearance personally. Other than the wear and tear that you should expect on the coat of a brood bitch that has just gone through pregnancy and puppy raising, the parents should look good.

Some colors within the American Pit Bull Terrier and American Staffordshire Terrier breeds may tend to have more skin problems than others. The dilute colors—blue, chocolate (or liver), and cream—may be more susceptible to skin worries than others. This is not always the case. However, dilute colors do, in all breeds where they occur, tend to prove out this hypothesis.

What you feed your pet may contribute to the presence of skin conditions. Some ingredients are said to produce rashes or hot spots in some dogs and even in some breeds.

Washing your APBT or Amstaff too often will promote a dry coat and flaky skin. In addition, poor housing and poorly maintained hygiene can contribute to skin problems. Stress and allergies to common household chemicals can cause skin and coat problems.

By and large, most American Pit Bull Terriers and most American Staffordshire Terriers are not plagued with the high percentages of allergic reactions and poor skin and coats with which some other breeds must contend. Choosing the right breeder and the right stock from which to pick your puppy will usually help you avoid most inherited skin concerns.

Some APBTs and Amstaffs will have severe reactions to insect bites. Bee stings and ant bites can cause excessive swelling and possible death for some dogs. Watch for these reactions, and rush your pet to the veterinarian.

Inherited Conditions

Because much of their fairly recent history involved the necessity for superb physical conditioning, both the American Staffordshire Terrier and the American Pit Bull Terrier do not have much of a legacy of poor inheritance. Because their ancestry had to survive under the toughest of circumstances, until the recent flush of popularity, these breeds did not have poor-quality specimens serving as breeding stock.

Some closely bred (line or inbred) strains or families may be more prone to some inherited problems. As mentioned, some families may tend to be more animal aggressive than others. This trait, which was highly desired during the pit days, must still be considered as an inherited condition. This, and other isolated family traits and inheritances, would almost be from strain to strain rather than representative of these breeds as a whole. Your breeder-mentor would be the best source of information about inherited traits and behaviors, good or bad, in the ancestry of the puppy that you choose.

Parasites

Internal Parasites

Roundworms: Roundworms can infest dogs of all ages even though puppies are most often the victims of this internal pest. The pups often have roundworms even before they are born, having gotten them from their mother prenatally.

Roundworms will sap the vigor and growth potential of little terrier pups. They siphon off a puppy's bright and shiny look and pull down its vitality. Youngsters simply cannot thrive when anchored down by these parasites.

Your veterinarian can rid your pups and their mother of these health robbers. You may discover roundworms in your pup's stool or vomitus. Seek immediate professional treatment.

Because good kennel hygiene can cut down on roundworm infestations, keep any areas the puppies share especially clean and sanitary. Get rid of stools quickly and appropriately. Pay close attention to kennel and home cleanliness. The larval forms of this parasite are transmissible to humans.

Hookworms: Hookworms, like roundworms, can be in evidence in dogs throughout their lives. Hookworms are also especially hard on puppies, who simply will not thrive while these worms are in them. Puppies with hookworms will have bloody stools, or their feces will appear very dark and tarlike.

Hookworms are little bloodsuckers that attach themselves to the insides of a puppy's small intestines. Pups with hookworms will sometimes become anemic. These parasites reduce a puppy's ability to fight off disease. As with all internal parasites, your veterinarian is the sworn enemy of hookworms

and will dispatch them for the good of your puppy.

Tapeworms: Tapeworms are a parasite brought by a parasite. Fleas are the host of tapeworms. When your dog has fleas, it can also have tapeworms. Your Amstaff or APBT will never be at its best while infested with tapeworms. Keep fleas off your dog and out of its environment, and then get tapeworms out of your dog.

Your veterinarian will be able to help you dispose of both parasitic problems—the fleas and the tapeworms. Because tapeworms can really hamper a puppy's growth and a dog's potential, get them and any other internal parasites treated as soon as possible.

Heartworms: The heartworm is another parasite that comes to you compliments of a pest. Heartworms are transmitted to your pet through infested mosquitoes. The mosquito bites your pet and deposits heartworm larvae onto your dog. These larvae enter the dog's bloodstream through the mosquito bite. Once in the dog's bloodstream, the larvae will ultimately make their way to the dog's heart. Once there, they will grow and increasingly clog this crucial organ until your pet is fatally affected.

Heartworms have expanded their territory thanks to their mosquito hosts. Today, a large part of the United States is threatened by heartworm infestation. The diagnosis for heartworms is made using a blood test. Your veterinarian will help you devise a plan to prevent heartworms from infesting your APBT or Amstaff or to treat an affected animal. The preventive plan will involve regular preventive testing and regular doses of preventive medicine that will kill heartworm larvae before they can enter the dog's heart.

Dogs with heartworms can be treated, but this is a risky, long, and expensive procedure. Prevention of heartworm problems is best for you and best for your dog!

External Parasites

Fleas: Fleas are the curse of many dogs' lives. They are the most common parasite affecting dogs. They literally feed on your dog's blood. In very severe infestations, fleas can cause anemic conditions in canines. Anemia can lead to death, especially in puppies. Fleas add insult to injury in that they are also the host and introducer of tapeworms into dogs.

Some dogs, like some humans, can have a severe allergic reaction to these pests. This fleabite allergy can cause severe scratching, hair loss, and absolute misery to the afflicted dog. This condition requires immediate treatment by a veterinarian to diagnose and treat the allergy. The owner will have to be absolutely fanatical about ridding the dog's living area of all fleas.

Dealing with fleas involves a take-no-prisoners mentality. The sooner you understand that fleas are your and your dog's mortal enemy and take charge of an eradication program, the sooner your pet will be safe from fleas. If your dog has fleas, fleas will be *everywhere* your dog can go. This will include your home, your yard, your car, the dog's kennel area, and so forth. If you fail to rid any of these places of all the fleas, eggs, and pupae that exist, you have failed in all the places—for the fleas will soon be back.

Consult with your veterinarian and with a knowledgeable pet products person to discover the weapons at your disposal to wipe fleas from the face of your dog's world. Flea dips, shampoos, collars, dusts, and sprays are on-dog weapons. Foggers, carpet cleaners, and in-home sprays take care of the dwelling. Yard sprays and kennel dust will stop the fleas that lie in wait outside the home. Remember to treat those places where the dog may go only sometimes: the car or the cottage at the lake.

Fleas spend 90 percent of their life cycle *off* your dog. Only the adult fleas, about 10 percent of the flea population, are actually on your pet. Deal with the 90 percent by using products designed for each area (always use great care and always follow the directions!). Your regular exterminator may also be able to help in large areas like your home and yard.

Ticks: Ticks are usually much larger than fleas and they can siphon off just that much more blood. Ticks will fill up on your dog's blood and will grow several times their original size. Their bites on a short-haired dog like the APBT and Amstaff can become unsightly scars. Tick bites also can become infected.

Ticks are not only a general nuisance; they can carry the life-threatening Lyme disease (see "Borelliosis," page 94) and other diseases, such as Rocky Mountain spotted fever, that can affect dogs and humans. Ticks can readily move from your dog, to your children, to you.

Fortunately, ticks do not seem to be the tough foe that fleas are. They can usually be controlled by the regular use of veterinary-recommended sprays, dips, powders, and flea-and-tick collars for on-dog use. You may also want to treat the living area with an antitick spray that will keep them from getting back onto your pet later.

CHECKLIST

Safely Removing a Tick from Your Dog

✔ Never simply pull a tick off your APBT/Amstaff. Doing so may leave part of the tick in your dog's skin, which cannot only be irritating but which could lead to a bad infection or even a bad scar.

✔ Place a small amount of rubbing alcohol precisely at the site of the tick's mouth and bite. Make sure that the alcohol does not get into your dog's eyes or mouth!

✔ With the dog being held or remaining still, carefully use tweezers to grasp the tick as close as possible to the dog's skin. *Very slowly* pull out the tick's mouth and head from the bite it made in your dog.

✔ Be certain to get any tick mouth parts carefully out of the bite. When you think you have removed all of the tick, put a little alcohol onto the bite or use another antiseptic to help prevent infection.

✔ When using the tweezers, be very careful that you do not do more damage to the dog than a tick bite. If a tick is deep in your pet's ear or very near an eye, let your veterinarian handle this tick removal.

✔ After a tick is removed, do not just drop it onto the ground. Ticks can get back onto a dog or another blood source. Dispose of the tick in a proper fashion. Because of the deer tick potential as a Lyme disease carrier, you should have all ticks positively identified.

✔ Sometimes you will see *two* ticks at one bite site. The larger of the two will be female, and she will be blood engorged. The smaller tick will be the male. Be sure to get all of both ticks carefully out of your dog's skin.

✔ Make regular inspections of your dog, especially on the shoulders, head, and ears after you have been in any environment where ticks may be able to get on your pet.

✔ Consider having your backyard or kennel area regularly sprayed with a veterinarian-approved product to reduce tick infestations.

✔ Prior to going for walks or hikes in areas where ticks may be lurking, spray some flea-and-tick spray onto your pet to reduce the chances of bringing some of these parasites home with you.

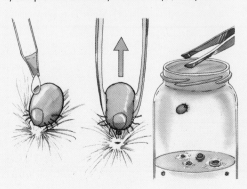

To remove a tick, place a drop of alcohol at the bite site. Slowly pull out all of the tick and dispose of it in a jar of alcohol or gasoline.

Ear mites: Your Amstaff's or APBT's ears can become the target of another external parasite, the ear mite. These microscopic little pests live both in the ear and in the ear canal. You can spot their presence by a dirty, waxy, dark residue on the skin inside the ear.

Ear mites can cause your dog a lot of discomfort. If you see your pet shaking its head from side to side in a violent manner, or if your dog constantly digs or scratches at its ears, ear mites are possibly to blame.

Although home remedies can stop these mites, always follow your veterinarian's preferred method of handling these parasites. As you look for ticks in your American Staffordshire Terrier's or APBT's ears, look for evidence of ear mites.

Mange: Two kinds of mange exist. Both are caused by a mite:

✔ Demodectic, or red, mange especially affects puppies and old dogs. Both of these ages are especially susceptible to the ragged and patchy appearance, especially around the head and face, that is commonly called mange. Red mange usually causes patchy hair loss around the eyes and face. Occasionally, it can cause severe hair loss and severe itching.

✔ Sarcoptic mange is also caused by a mite. This one burrows into your dog's skin. It usually causes significant hair loss and intense scratching that can make unsightly raw wounds on a dog's skin, which can become infected. Sarcoptic mange mites can also live temporarily on humans, causing an itchy rash.

Your veterinarian can provide a treatment plan for both kinds of mange and keep your pet from the ugly, uncomfortable, and unhealthy side effects of these tiny mites.

Emergency Care

Accidents

Do everything you can to prevent accidents, but know that even the best dog owner cannot anticipate every situation where an accident could occur. The primary rule in trying to help an injured pet is *do not make things worse!* You could get bitten yourself if you carelessly approach even a trusted pet who is confused, in pain, and frightened. If you are injured, that will delay the help you need to get for your dog. Your first step is to find some way to muzzle and immobilize your pet so that it will not hurt you or itself.

Do not be in too much of a rush to move a nonmoving pet. Rough treatment can cause a relatively minor injury to become a severe or even fatal injury. Remember that you are your pet's best hope only if you act rationally.

If your Amstaff or American Pit Bull Terrier is involved in a fight, remember that these breeds are more likely to make use of their powerful jaws to grab on, hold on, and shake the opponent. If the other dog is some breed other than an Amstaff or an APBT, you are more likely to be bitten by the other dog, as you try to separate them than by your dog.

Heatstroke

The most ludicrous way for a dog to die is for its owner to leave it in a parked car on a day when the outside temperature is 60°F (15.6°C) or more. The metal of the car and the heat-increasing properties of auto glass can turn the family sedan into an oven of death for a pet left there for even a few minutes!

Clinical signs of heatstroke include a dazed look and rapid, shallow panting with a high fever. The dog's gums will be bright red.

Speed is crucial if a dog is in this condition. *Act immediately.* Lower your pet's temperature by pouring a mixture of cool water and rubbing alcohol all over the dog's body, then transport your pet to the nearest veterinarian!

Bleeding

The first thing to do when a dog is bleeding is to identify the source of the bleeding. After you are sure that you have the source and not just a bloody spot, apply firm, but gentle, pressure to the wound with your hand. If the wound is on an extremity (front legs, back legs, tail), place a tourniquet between the injury and the dog's heart. Loosen the tourniquet for 30 to 60 seconds every 15 minutes. If the bleeding continues, if the dog has lost a significant amount of blood, or if the dog has a gaping wound, consult your veterinarian as soon as possible!

Recognizing Potential Poisons

Your American Pit Bull Terrier or American Staffordshire Terrier can be hurt in many ways, but one of the riskiest places is right in your home. Modern life provides many opportunities for a pet to ingest some deadly drug or chemical.
✔ Antifreeze is fatal to dogs, and it has a sweet taste that attracts them. Spilled or leaked antifreeze may be hard to spot, but your pet can find it.
✔ Chocolate can kill a dog or puppy if eaten in sufficient quantity.
✔ A number of yard and garden plants are dangerous to pets, especially to young pups that enjoy chewing on things. Favorites such as azalea, rhododendron, and holly can kill a young dog. Wild plants like mistletoe and poison ivy can cause severe, even fatal, reactions in some dogs. Check with your local county

extension service for a list of poisonous plants that thrive where you live.
✔ Houseplants like dieffenbachia, poinsettia, and jade plants can all be killers. Ask your extension service about a list of local favorites, and check out any houseplant's poison potential before you bring it into your home.
✔ Keep all insecticides, pesticides, garden and lawn chemicals, and cleaning solvents away from places your Amstaff or APBT can prowl.

If your dog suddenly becomes listless, convulses, seems disoriented, or is unconscious, it may be a victim of poison. Other signs of poisoning include a change in color of the mucous membranes, vomiting, and diarrhea. The presence of these signs is worth a trip to the veterinarian that may save your pet's life!

Areas Requiring Lifelong Attention

Teeth

Your APBT or Amstaff will depend greatly on its teeth all its life. These dogs put even greater pressure onto their teeth than do most other breeds. Unless you pay close attention to your dog's choppers beginning when it is a very young puppy, teeth problems could become a source of pain, discomfort, unpleasant breath, or even life-threatening infections. Dental care for dogs cannot just be turned over to your veterinarian during your twice-yearly, regular visits. As with humans, the care of your Amstaff's or APBT's mouth, gums, and teeth should be a daily activity.

Caring for Your Dog's Teeth
✔ Regular inspections will alert you to any abnormalities. Every day, as you pet or play

Cleaning your dog's teeth on a regular basis will help prevent plaque buildup and tooth decay:

with your American Pit Bull Terrier or American Staffordshire Terrier, take just a moment to settle the pet down to look at its mouth.

✔ Look at the teeth, gums, throat, and lips not just for tooth decay but for the presence of tartar and foreign objects (like pieces of wood or bone from the dog's chewing habits).

✔ Pay attention to tartar as it can bring on gum disease and tooth decay. It also makes the dog's mouth look bad.

✔ Start very early with the Amstaff or APBT puppy to clean its teeth. As with so many other areas of dog ownership, the earlier you start it, the easier it will be!

✔ To clean your pet's teeth, use veterinarian-approved brushes and utensils and a toothpaste designed for dogs, not humans. Canine teeth cleaning is not difficult if you can get the pet to come to enjoy or accept it early. Teeth cleaning will also largely involve brushing if you begin the practice with a puppy and continue it often and regularly. Two or three times a week is good; daily brushing is even better.

✔ Tartar scraping is never pleasant and comes as a result of neglecting your dog's teeth. This severe tartar removal procedure may have to be done at the veterinarian's.

✔ Schedule regular veterinary dental checkups with occasional professional teeth cleaning to catch any areas you may have missed.

✔ Use veterinarian-approved and experienced Amstaff/APBT breeder-reviewed chew toys and dental exercisers to help keep tartar at a minimum.

Note: Remember that chew toys and other similar items designed for the average dog may *not* be adequate for your American Pit Bull Terrier or American Staffordshire Terrier. If your APBT demolishes inappropriate chewing devices, pieces could be swallowed and necessitate surgery to remove them from the dog's intestines.

✔ The only adequate way to clean your pet's teeth is through regular care by you and regular cleaning by a professional. Dog biscuits, chew toys, and rawhide strips are no substitute for good home care and professional attention.

Eyes

Your APBT or Amstaff does not have the large, prominent eyes of some breeds. This fact does not mean that these dogs will be immune to eye injuries or eye problems. Often dogs of these breeds are very exuberant and active. Such love of life can cause a pet to not notice possible eye-injuring situations. As the pet owner, you must help prevent these injuries. You can do so in several ways:

✔ In places where your pet is allowed to play or run, be alert for sharp pointed things the dog might not see, like thorns, briars, barbed

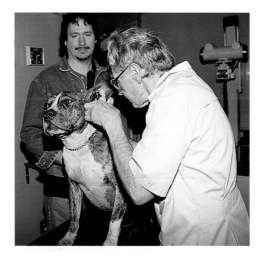

wire, stems, and rosebushes (especially those that may have been recently trimmed and are just at a dog's eye level).

✔ Caution children about throwing stones, playing with air rifles, and other activities that could be injurious to a curious pet's eyes.

✔ Keep your pet from chemically harming its eyes by avoiding places where considerable air pollution is taking place or where recent or residual chemical spraying could be on grass or shrubs and get into your pet's eyes.

Any ear disorder in your APBT/Amstaff should be brought to the attention of your veterinarian.

✔ Do not let your pet ride with its head out of an automobile window.

✔ Check your dog's eyes every day for injuries, foreign matter, reddening, or infection. You may notice that mucus sometimes appears in the corners of your American Staffordshire or APBT's eyes. Normally, this is perfectly natural and can simply be gently removed a soft cloth. This mucus should not be confused with a discharge that needs veterinary attention.

Ears

Your APBT or Amstaff can have either cropped ears (see the UKC and AKC breed standards, page 10) or uncropped (natural) ears. Although it is admittedly more difficult for an uncropped show dog to win against cropped dogs, it does frequently happen.

Cropping American Pit Bull Terriers and American Staffordshire Terriers is very different from the ear surgery performed on Great Danes, Dobermans, and some others. Originally a protection against ear injuries in the pit, the medium-length crop now used on Amstaffs and APBTs is not as short as its pit predecessors but not nearly as long as that of the Dane and Dobe.

Cropping is largely a matter of personal preference. This cosmetic surgery is usually done by a veterinarian when the puppy is a couple of months old. Not every veterinarian

Ear problems can often go undetected by owners, so again, regular veterinary visits are important for proper diagnosis.

Prompt veterinary care for worms and other parasites can help your APBT/Amstaff stay healthy.

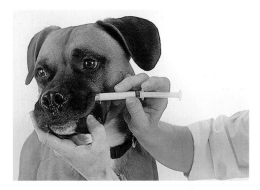

will want to, or will even know how to, crop in a way that fits current show preferences. Consult your breed mentor and other APBT or Amstaff breeders for recommendations.

Cropped or uncropped ears will still need daily inspection for injuries, infection, or infestations by ear mites or ticks (see page 94). Pay attention to the inside and the outside of the dog's ears. Keep young children, as well as sticks and toys, away from a dog's ears.

Feet and Toenails

Your American Pit Bull Terrier or American Staffordshire Terrier usually has sturdy feet, well able to support a sturdy medium-sized dog. However, every dog can sometimes have foot problems.

City living poses particular hazards. Running over paved surfaces can keep the toenails worn down where they may not need much trimming. In addition, city-dwelling APBTs and Amstaffs will suffer more damage to the pads of their feet from the rough, unyielding surfaces of concrete, paving stone, and asphalt. Bruises and abrasions are more often seen in this environment. Salt on winter sidewalks can also irritate a dog's feet.

The rural APBT or Amstaff will not miss out on foot concerns either. Constantly walking or running in a grassy backyard will not wear

Administering medicines properly, recognizing warning signs for illness, and giving your pet regular at-home exams can add years to your dog's life.

down nails, and these will grow too long unless you trim them. Splinters, thorns, slivers of broken glass, and even small stones can get between a pet's toes or into the soft tissue of the pad and cause trouble.

Daily inspections of your dog's feet will prevent most minor conditions from becoming major problems. Trimming your dog's toenails, like brushing its teeth, must be started early to be easily accomplished. You need a good set of canine nail clippers. These can be either the scissors or the guillotine type. As your dog's nails grow, trim back just the tip on each nail. Do not cut too deeply or the quick, or blood

supply to the nail, will be injured and may bleed. Following trimming, smooth the edges of the nail with a nail file or an emery board.

Administering Medicine

You should know how to administer the prescriptions your veterinarian gives you to keep your pet healthy or to help it regain its health. This activity is not always as easy as it sounds. Like a lot of American Pit Bull Terrier or American Staffordshire Terrier care, it should start while the animal is still a puppy.

Some dogs just do not like to be dosed with medicine. They will spit out capsules or tablets. Some dog owners will hide a pill in a treat in order to get it down.

A more direct approach and one that can be used when a dog may catch on to the treat trick is to:

1. Speak calmly and reassuringly as you open the dog's mouth.

2. Tilt its head back only slightly.

3. Place the pill as far back onto the dog's tongue as possible (or in the case of liquid medicine, pour it over the back of the tongue).

CHECKLIST

Helping an Injured Pet

✔ Remain calm yourself. Your pet will pick up on your anxiety if you let it show.

✔ Speak to the pet in a calm, confident voice to reassure it that you are here to take the hurt away. Your dog will usually have confidence in you that you can make things all right.

✔ Move very slowly, making no sudden moves that could alarm an injured and frightened animal.

✔ Even if this dog is your lifelong pal, muzzle it gently but securely. An APBT- or Amstaff-sized muzzle might be a good investment just in case of injuries, but a necktie, leash, or belt might also work.

✔ After the dog is muzzled, immediately attend to any bleeding (see "Bleeding," page 102).

✔ Be very supportive when you try to move an adult American Staffordshire or American Pit Bull Terrier. If you can get someone else to help you, certainly do so. If you can get something, such as a door or wide board, to serve as a safe and secure stretcher, use it.

✔ If you are alone, you may have to use your coat, a piece of carpet, or a tarp to devise a way for you to move the pet safely, gently sliding the dog along if you cannot or if it is not advisable to lift it.

✔ Call your veterinarian, or have someone else do it, to alert the clinic of the injury and of your arrival time.

✔ Drive *safely* to the veterinarian. You are more likely to make things worse by driving recklessly.

✔ Follow the age-old medical precept "First, do no harm" in all of your actions designed to help an injured pet.

4. Gently but firmly close the dog's mouth, holding the jaws closed with your hand, and continue to talk to the dog until it swallows the medicine.

Always remember to follow the veterinarian's instructions, dosages, and medication schedule carefully. Never give your APBT or Amstaff human medicines or remedies without your veterinarian's prior approval.

When Your APBT/Amstaff Grows Older

These breeds have a good, long life span and may be with you and your family well into their teens. Gradually, that humorous, innocent puppy that became that powerful APBT or Amstaff will turn into a gray-muzzled senior. Normally, a dog of these breeds will age well and keep both its good health and its devotion to its humans.

The oldster will sleep a little more, play a little less. It will still want to be included in family activities and not be replaced by a younger and more vigorous puppy. All of the teeth, eyes, ears, feet, and toenail care take on added importance with a distinguished veteran. Your visits to the veterinarian may come a little more often as your pet's health needs change.

You will need to be certain that the dog is fed a good senior dog food that will not contribute to obesity, a condition that will really hurt an older pet. Your pet may need a little less food and a few more frequent walks and visits to the relief spot. Although slower, more willing to watch than participate, but still desperately in need of your loving touch and approval, your older pet will still have as much

affection for you and your family as it ever had. You will need to be sure that your old dog knows that you still love it too.

Saying Good-bye (Euthanasia)

That inquisitive, little Amstaff or APBT that won your heart at the breeder's will make way for the frisky adolescent and then the sturdy adult. Over the years, this American Staffordshire or American Pit Bull Terrier will have become a trusted and greatly loved member of your family.

One day your APBT/Amstaff may begin a downward slide in health and activity. Under ideal circumstances, your pet would be relatively healthy one day and then quietly and painlessly die in its sleep that night.

In most cases, though, barring fatal accidents or injuries, an old dog will just grow older and older until age and infirmity makes its existence one of pain and anguish. It is at this point that the hardest decision a pet owner will ever have to make must be made.

When the life of your loving Amstaff or APBT becomes void of the fun of former times and when the dog looks to you with imploring eyes for an explanation for all the pain and physical incapacity, your decision must be one based on the best interests of the dog. Your veterinarian and your breed-mentor, now hopefully old friends to both you and your Amstaff or APBT, can be consulted. Euthanasia will be a gentle end to a full and happy life that has taken on very painful aspects. Ultimately, the decision is yours and it will never be easy. However, a time comes when you grasp all the positive memories, hold them tight, and then say good-bye to a dear and devoted friend.

INFORMATION

International Kennel Clubs and Breed Clubs

Staffordshire Terrier Club of America
Richard Pascoe, M.D.
785 Valley View Road
Forney, Texas 75126

National American Pit Bull Terrier Association
Todd Phipps
e-mail address: b3nut@mail.tds.net
Anna Burke Harris
e-mail address: annabh@swcp.com

American Kennel Club
260 Madison Avenue
New York, New York 10016

The American Dog Breeders Association
Box 1771
Salt Lake City, Utah 84110

United Kennel Club, Inc.
100 East Kilgore Road
Kalamazoo, Michigan 49001

Rescue and Breeder Referral Organizations

Staffordshire Terrier Club of America Breeder
   Referral
Sharon Gregory, Chairperson
1431 New York Avenue
Columbus, New Jersey 08022

Books

Alderton, David. *The Dog Care Manual.*
   Hauppauge, New York: Barron's Educational
   Series, Inc., 1986.
Baer, Ted. *Communicating with Your Dog.*
   Hauppauge, New York: Barron's Educational
   Series, Inc., 1989.
Klever, Ulrich. *The Complete Book of Dog Care.*
   Hauppauge, New York: Barron's Educational
   Series, Inc., 1990.
Ullman, Hans. *The New Dog Handbook.*
   Hauppauge, New York: Barron's Educational
   Series, Inc., 1984.
Wrede, Barbara. *Civilizing Your Puppy.*
   Hauppauge, New York: Barron's Educational
   Series, Inc., 1992.

A healthy, well-bred, well-socialized APBT/Amstaff puppy in a home where it will receive lots of love and good care is the best end product of dog breeding!